Street by Street

ALDERSHOT, CAMBERLEY, FARNHAM
FARNBOROUGH, FLEET

Ash, Bagshot, Bentley, Bisley, Blackwater, Brookwood, Cove, Crowthorne, Frimley, Lightwater, Rowledge, Sandhurst, Yateley

C000294948

2nd edition April 2005
© Automobile Association Developments Limited 2005

Original edition printed September 2002

Ordnance Survey® This product includes map data licensed from Ordnance Survey® with the permission of the Controller of Her Majesty's Stationery Office. © Crown copyright 2005. All rights reserved. Licence number 399221.

Published by AA Publishing (a trading name of Automobile Association Developments Limited, whose registered office is Southwood East, Apollo Rise, Farnborough, Hampshire, GU14 0JW. Registered number 1878835).

Mapping produced by the Cartography Department of The Automobile Association. (A02244)

A CIP Catalogue record for this book is available from the British Library.

Printed by GRAFIASA S.A., Porto, Portugal

Ref: ML164z

Key to map symbols	ii
Key to map pages	1
Enlarged map pages	2-5
Main map pages	6-63
Index – towns & villages	64
Index – streets	64-72
Index – featured places	72-73
Acknowledgements	73

Junction 9	Motorway & junction	Mounds		Cinema	
Services	Motorway service area	17	Page continuation 1:15,000	Golf course	
	Primary road single/dual carriageway	2	Page continuation to enlarged scale 1:10,000	Camping AA inspected	
Services	Primary road service area		River/canal, lake, pier	Caravan site AA inspected	
	A road single/dual carriageway		Aqueduct, lock, weir	Camping & caravan site AA inspected	
	B road single/dual carriageway	465 Winter Hill	Peak (with height in metres)	Theme park	
	Other road single/dual carriageway		Beach	Abbey, cathedral or priory	
	Minor/private road, access may be restricted		Woodland	Castle	
	One-way street		Park	Historic house or building	
	Pedestrian area		Cemetery	Wakehurst Place NT	National Trust property
	Track or footpath		Built-up area	M	Museum or art gallery
	Road under construction		Featured building		Roman antiquity
	Road tunnel		City wall		Ancient site, battlefield or monument
P	Parking	A&E	Hospital with 24-hour A&E department		Industrial interest
P+	Park & Ride	PO	Post Office		Garden
	Bus/coach station		Public library		Garden Centre Garden Centre Association Member
	Railway & main railway station	i	Tourist Information Centre		Garden Centre Wyevale Garden Centre
	Railway & minor railway station	i	Seasonal Tourist Information Centre		Arboretum
	Underground station		Petrol station, 24 hour Major suppliers only		Farm or animal centre
	Light railway & station	†	Church/chapel		Zoological or wildlife collection
	Preserved private railway		Public toilets		Bird collection
LC	Level crossing		Toilet with disabled facilities		Nature reserve
	Tramway	PH	Public house AA recommended	V	Visitor or heritage centre
	Ferry route		Restaurant AA inspected		Country park
	Airport runway	Madeira Hotel	Hotel AA inspected		Cave
	County, administrative boundary		Theatre or performing arts centre		Windmill
					Distillery, brewery or vineyard

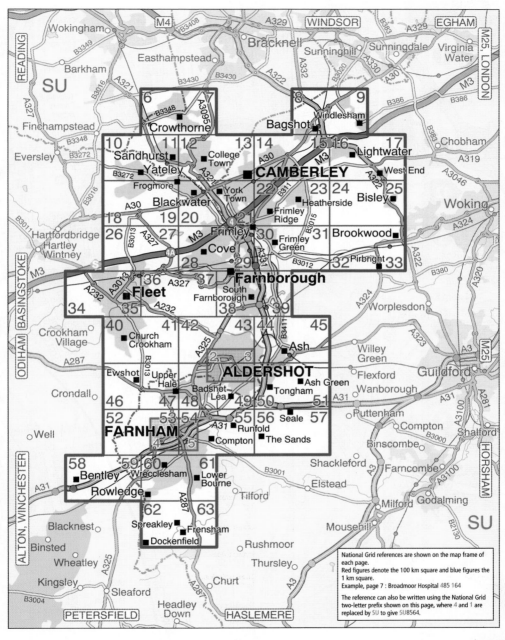

National Grid references are shown on the map frame of each page.
Red figures denote the 100 km square and blue figures the 1 km square.
Example, page 7 : Broadmoor Hospital 485 164

The reference can also be written using the National Grid two-letter prefix shown on this page, where 4 and 1 are replaced by SU to give SU8564.

Scale of enlarged map pages 1:10,000

6.3 inches to 1 mile

| 0 | miles | 1/4 |
| 0 | kilometres | 1/4 | 1/2 |

Scale of main map pages 1:15,000

4.2 inches to 1 mile

| 0 | 1/4 | miles | 1/2 |
| 0 | 1/4 | kilometres | 3/4 |

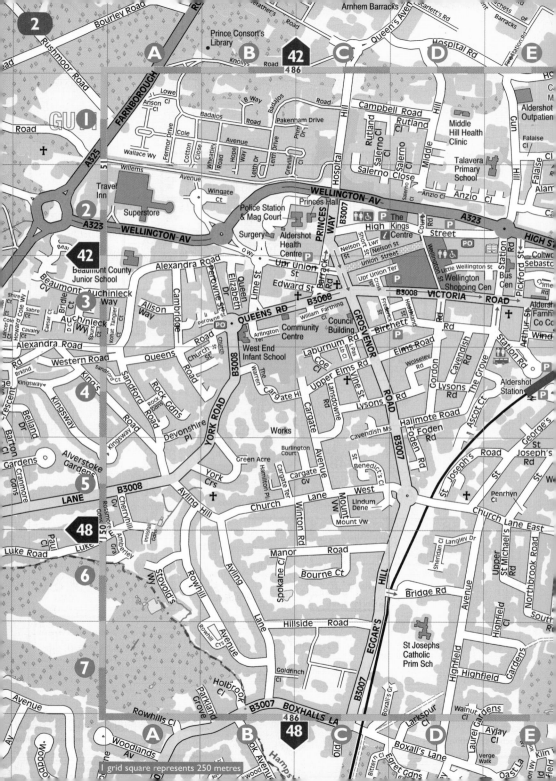

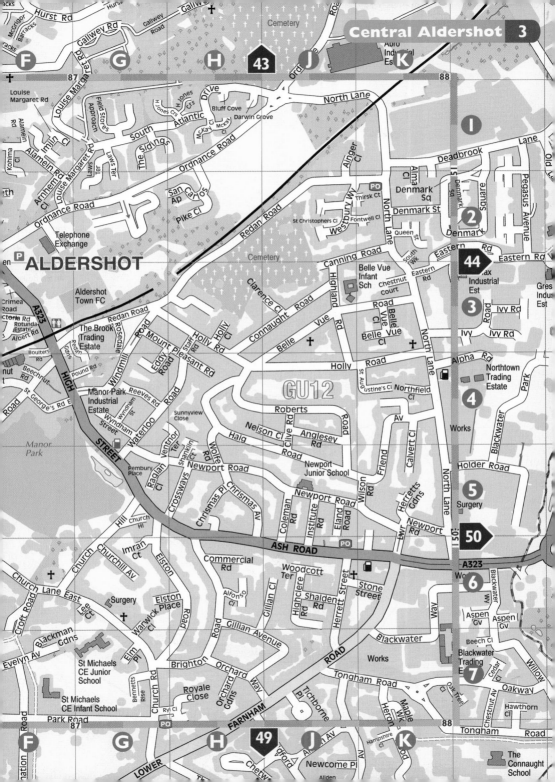

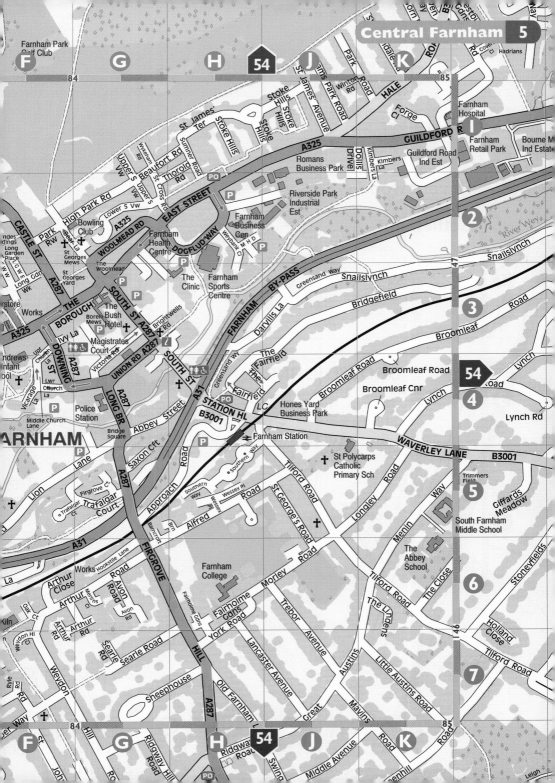

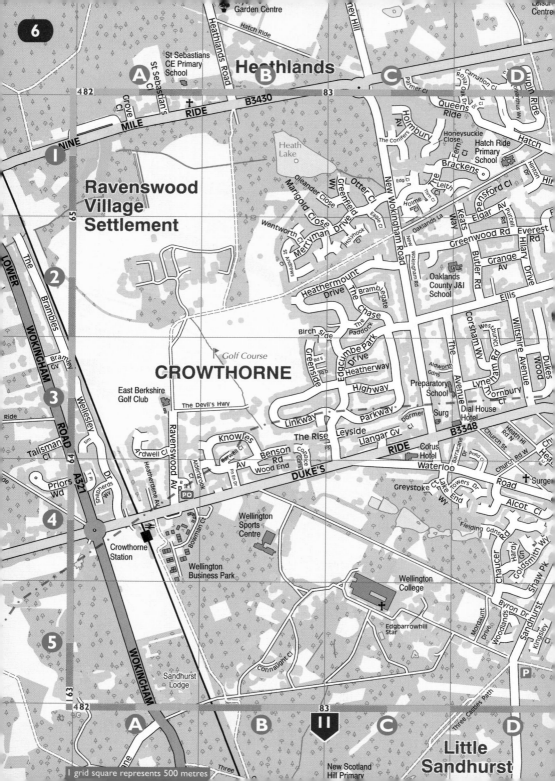

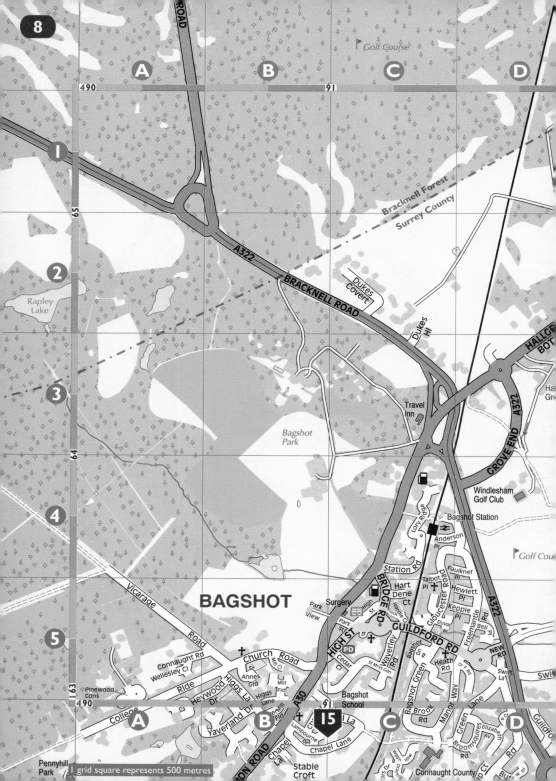

Country
Gardens
Estate

Wyevale
Garden
Centre

E F G H

Windlesham
Hall

LONDON ROAD

A30

Snows
Paddock

Windlesham Court

Westwood Road

I

65

2

Erl Wood
Manor

PH

Ross Tea

Cohing

SUNNINGHILL RD

Bosman Dr

Bosman

Chewter La

Newark Road

Popular Avenue

SCHOOL

Hawkes Leap

Newark Rd

Turpins Rd

Turpins Rise

Mill Pond Rd

Fosters Gv

Highwayman's Rdg

Leycester Cl

Wynsham WY

Mill

Pond Rd

White Hl

Moor Pl

Ride

Windlesham Court

Windlesham Village
Infant School

Woodcote
House
School

Snows

Hatton Hill

Hatton Hill

Westwood Road

3

94

Kings Lane

Ramsay Rd

Owen Rd

Kent Rd

Caldwell Rd

Hinds

CHERTSEY RD

GU20

ROAD

B386

Hatton Hill

KENNEL LANE

Cochrane Rd

Covett

Cooper Rd

Baigents La

Cricketers La

School La

Atfield
Grove

Windle Close

Oakwood Road

Heathpark Drive

Birch

Edward Road

4

WINDLESHAM

New Road

Church Road

Birch Hall

Rectory Lane

Hatch
End

Pound Lane

UPDOWN HILL

Bytes Gv

Graham Rd

Lawn Crt

Split Gn

Windmill Field

Prm

PO

Uptown Rd

Thorndown Lane

Broadley Green

Pine Grove

163

5

M3

Hutton Cl

Orchard
Hl

Works

Ashleigh
Farm

Broadway Road

E F G H

93 16 94

Junction 3

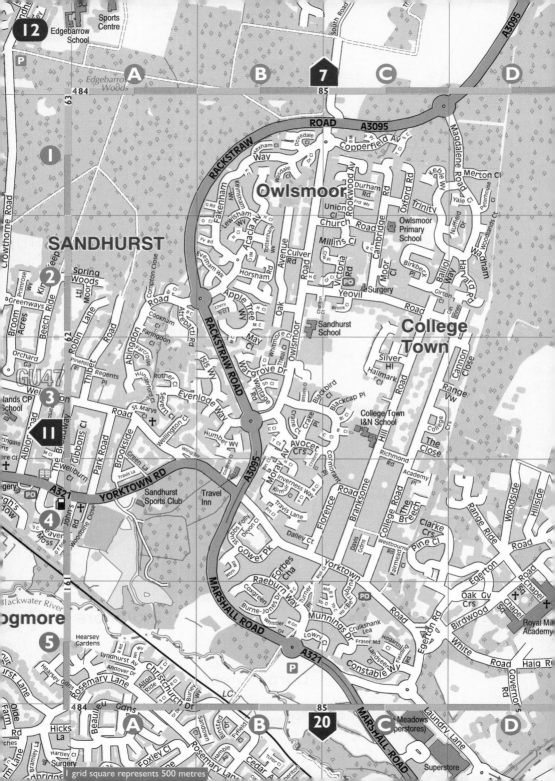

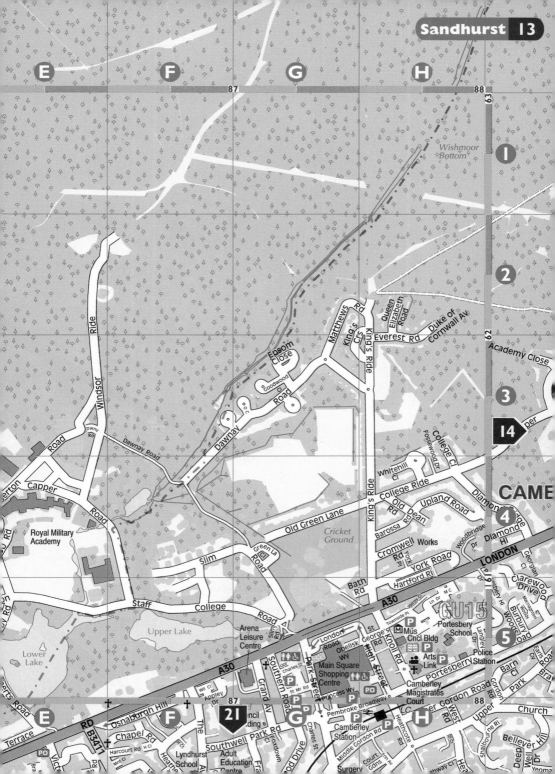

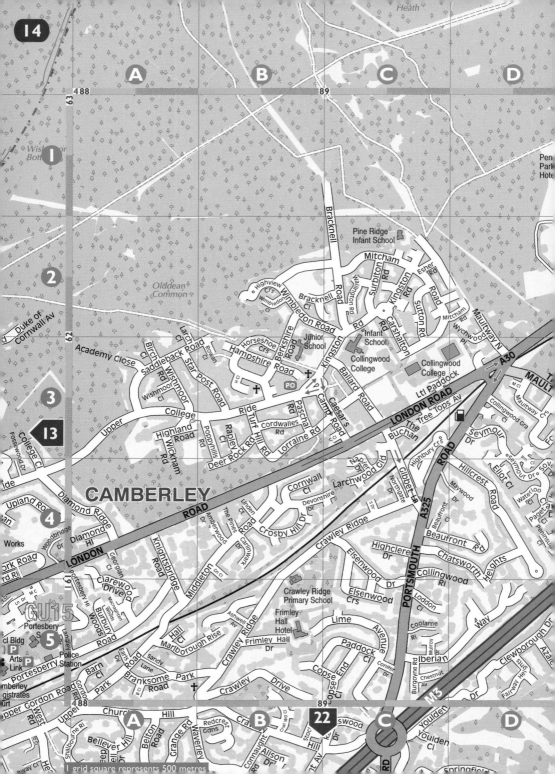

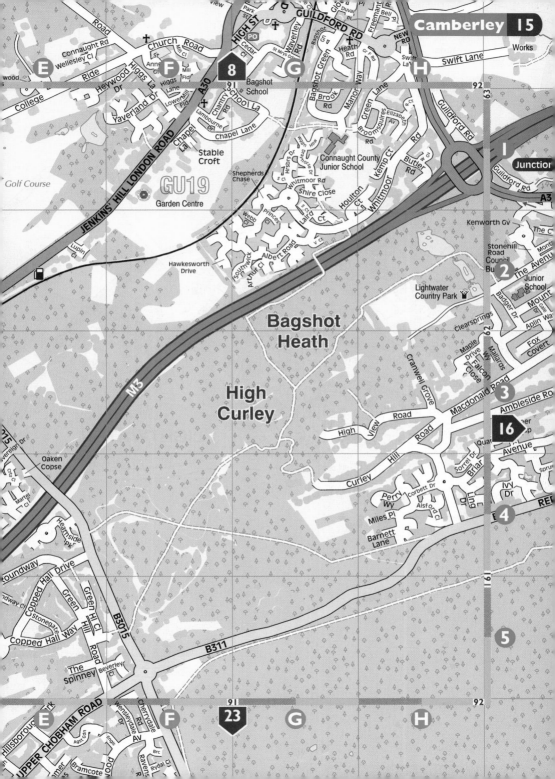

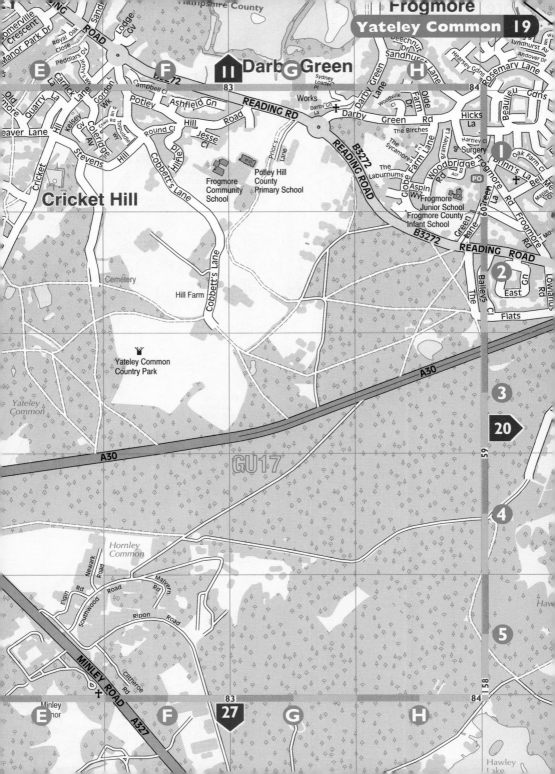

Somerville Crescent

Manor Park Dr

Royal Oak Close

Peddlars Gv

Lodge Gv

SANDH... ROAD

83

II **Darby Green** G

Sydney Loader Pl

Campbell Cl

Ashfield Gn

READING RD

Works

Darby Cn La

Darby Green

+ Darby

Hampshire County

Beechnut Dr

Lyndhurst Av

Andover Rd

Hearsey Gdns

Sandhurst Lane

Darby Green Lane

Woodville Cl

Olde Farm Dr

Green Rd

Rosemary Lane

Beaulieu Gdns

H

Carrick Lane

Quarry Hill

Kelsey Gv

Gordon Wk

Coleridge Av

Potley Hill Road

Round Cl

Hill

Jesse Cl

Cobbett's Lane

B3272

Prior's Lane

READING ROAD

B3272

The Birches

The Sycamores

Bramley Rd

Hartley Cl

Surgery

The Laburnums

Glebe Farm Lane

Aspin WY

Close Farm Lane

Woodbridge Rd

Acr Rd

PO

Frogmore Green Lane

Brinn's La

Hicks La

Bell

Oak Farm Cl

I

+

Cricket Hill

Stevens Hill

Hillfield

Frogmore Community School

Potley Hill County Primary School

Frogmore Junior School

Frogmore County Infant School

Frogmore Rd

Lowlandes Rd

2

East Gn

Baileys Lane

84

READING ROAD

B3272

The Flats

Cemetery

Hill Farm

Cobbett's Lane

3

Yateley Common Country Park

A30

20

Yateley Common

A30

GU17

59

4

Hornley Common

Newark Road

Elgin Rd

Southwood Road

Malvern Rd

Ripon Road

Haw

Hawley Lake

5

Minley Manor

X

MINLEY ROAD

Clitheroe Rd

A327

158

E

83

27

F

G

H

84

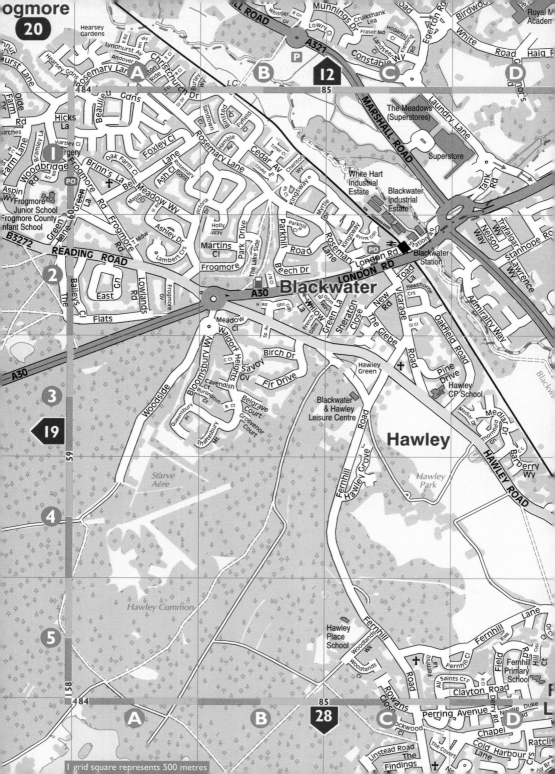

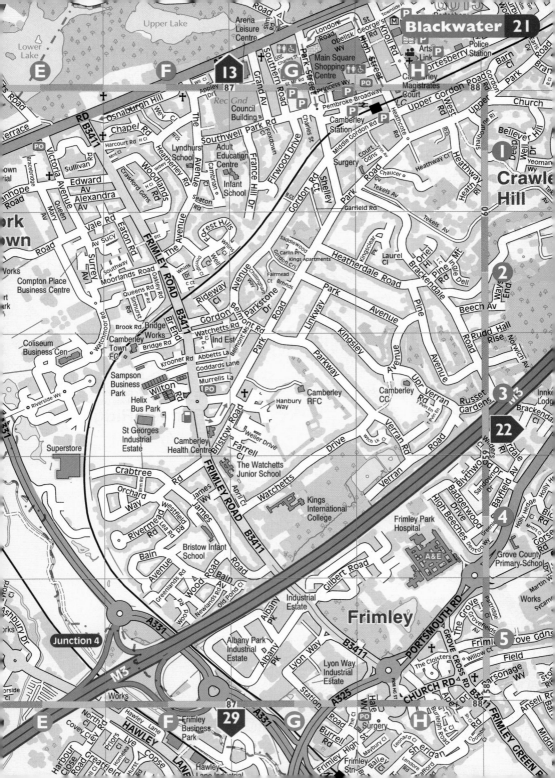

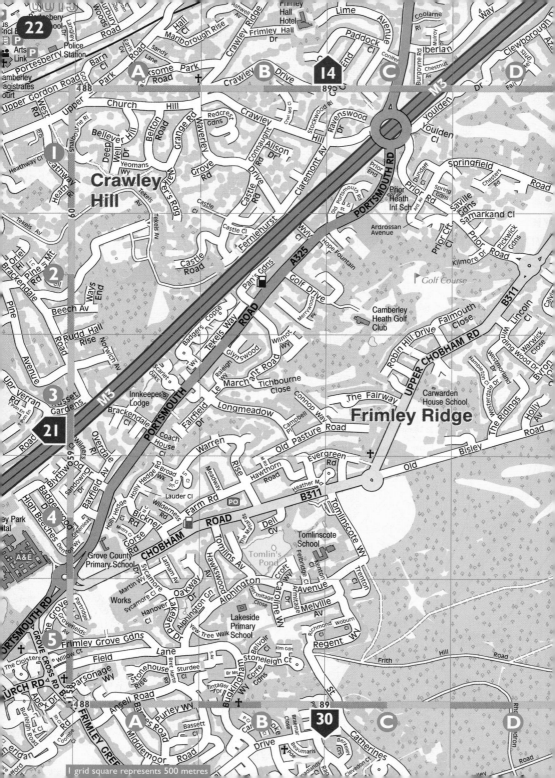

Copped Hall Way
Stonegate
B3015
Hi Cl
Hill
Road
B311

E
The
Spinney
Beverley
Cl
F
15
G
H

Hillsborough Park
UPPER CHOBHAM ROAD
Wensleydale Dr
Cherrydale Rd
Agar Cdn
Engli
Rydal Cl
I

Summer Gdns
Bramcote
Dawsmere Cl
Brc
1

Langdon Close
Norton Walk
Margal Cl
Ravenstone Rd
Gfhn
Inglewood
Buttermere Dr
2

Tremayne
AV
Eskdale Way
Copelands Close
Drive
Kendal Cl
Strawberry Bottom

Surgery
Keswick Cl
Road
Arundel Road

Cumberland
PO
Heather Ridge County Infant School
2

Roxburgh Close
Bellingham
Brandon Cl
Martindale Avenue
Kirkstone Close
Redwood Drive

eatherside
Chevi ot Close
Constable
Pendragon Way
Shildon Cl
Yockley Close

Silver
Herrick Cl
Theobal ds Way
Barbon Close
Ripon Close
Dalston Close
3

Edgemoor Rd
Maguire Dr
MAULTWAY
24

Old
Ridgeway
Cheviesmore
Wingfield Gdns
Drive
Habershon
B3015
3

Bisley
Road
59
4

Pine Ridge Golf Club
Colony Gate

Golf Course

DEEPCUT BRIDGE ROAD
Minorca Av
Minorca Road
5

Alsne Road

Hill
Road
B3015
92
58

alley Road
Drifters Dr
Crofters Cl
Swordsman's Rd
E
F
angen Crs
31
G
Alma Gardens
H

Earl P.Chester Dr
Sutton Cl
straw
Malta Road
Canada Rd
Dettingen Road

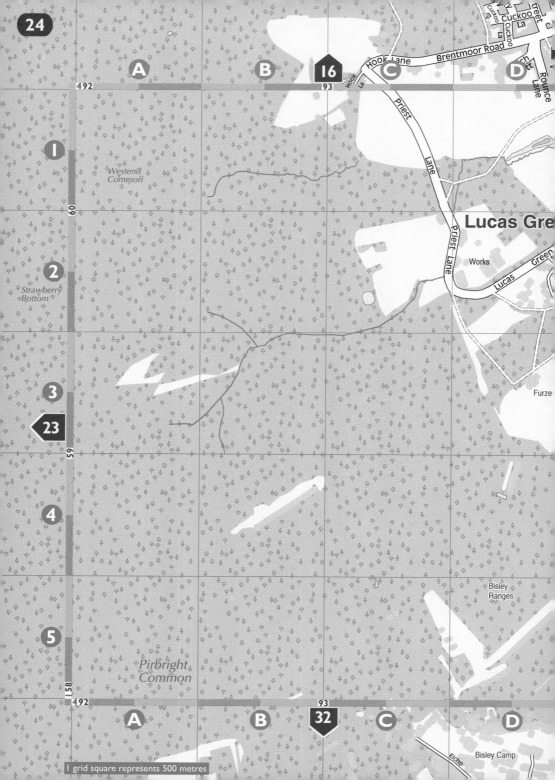

24

A B **16** C D

492 93 Hook La Hook Lane Brentmoor Road Cuckoo La Cuckoo La Rounce La

I Westend Common Priest Lane

60 **Lucas Gre**

2 Strawberry Bottom Works Lucas Green

3 Furze

59 **◄23**

4 Bisley Ranges

5 Pirbright Common

158 492 93 **32** Elcho Bisley Camp

A B C D

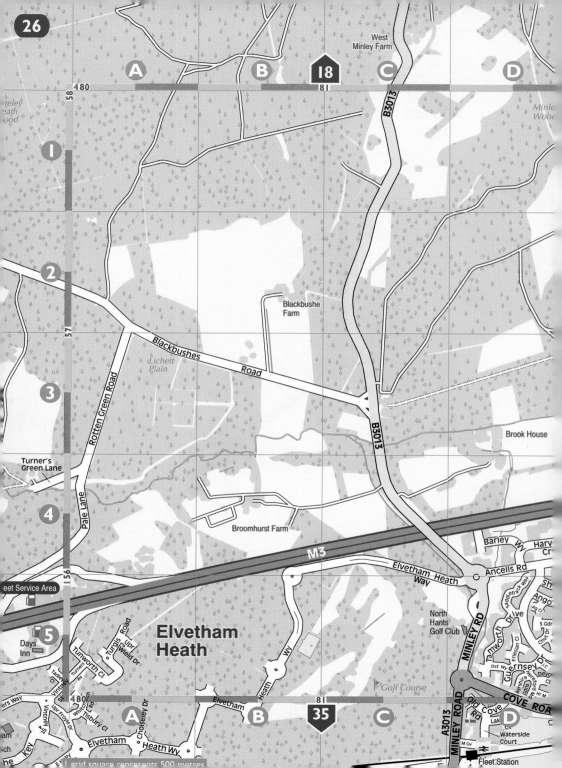

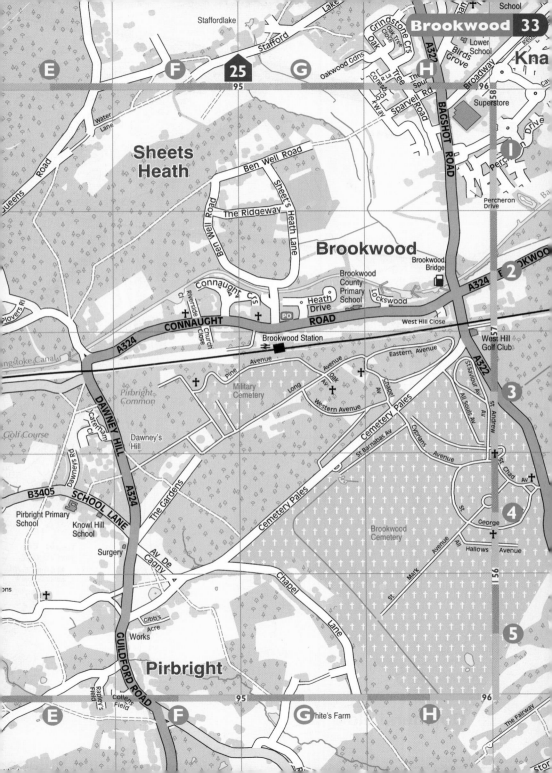

E F **25** G H Kna

Staffordlake

Stafford

Lake

Grindstone Crs
Oak Tree Close
Oakwood Gdns
Oak Tree Way

Birds Grove
Lower School
Broadway

A322

Superstore

Water Lane

Sheets Heath

Ben Well Road

Sheet's Heath Lane

The Ridgeway

Ben Well Road

Queens Road

Connaught Crs

Riverside Close

Church Close

Sparvell Rd
The Spur

Brookwood

Brookwood County Primary School

Heath Drive

PO

Brookwood Bridge

Lockswood

Percheron Drive

I

A324

OKWO 2

CONNAUGHT ROAD

West Hill Close

West Hill Golf Club

Plovers Rd

A324

Brookwood Station

Pine Avenue

Long Avenue

Oak Av.

Western Avenue

Eastern Avenue

Chapel Av.

All Souls Av.

St Saviour Av

A322

St Andrew Av.

3

Pirbright Common

Military Cemetery

Cemetery Pales

St Barnabas Av

St Cyprians Avenue

St Chad Av

Golf Course

Caterham Cl

Dawney's Hill

Dawneys Rd

DAWNEY HILL

St Andrew

A324

The Gardens

Cemetery Pales

Brookwood Cemetery

St George

4

B3405

SCHOOL LANE

Pirbright Primary School

Knowl Hill School

Surgery

Av De Cagny

Chapel Lane

St Mark Avenue

All Hallows Avenue

5

Gibb's Acre

Works

GUILDFORD ROAD

Pirbright

Rapley's Field

Collers Field

E F 95 G hite's Farm H 96

The Fairway

Days Inn

A 478 **B** 79 **C** **D**

Kingsley Sq

Palelane Farm

Kimpton Drive

Mounts

Kings Worthy Rd

Lyndhurst Rd

Lower Mount Street

Emery Down

Way

Ramsdell Cl

Turners Way

Vintney St

Eversley Dri

Elvetham Crs

Elvetham Heath Prim Sch

The Key

Chawton Cl

Chineham Cl

Elvetham Heath

Elvetham Heath

Elvetham Heath

Alfre

1 55

2 55

Pale Lane

Elvetham Road

West Hj Cdns

READING ROAD N

A3²

Broomrig Road

Glendale Pk

Fitzroy Road

Bl Cl

Perry Dr

3 54

Wh Ct

Barley Mow Close

The Oaks

Dukes

Mead

Mns Rd

Priory Cl

Tavistock

Woodcote Gn

Du

Calthorpe Park School

Snld Wy

Road

Tavistock

Brdcr

Me

4

Hart Sports Centre

Tavistock Infant School

All Saints CE Junior School

New Barn

Larmer Cl

Larme Cl

Nethethouse

5 53

Hitches Lane

Swan Way

Hawkll GV

Dogmersfield CE Primary School

478

79

A Dog▪ersfield PH **B** **C** **D**

Pilcot Road

Crookham Village

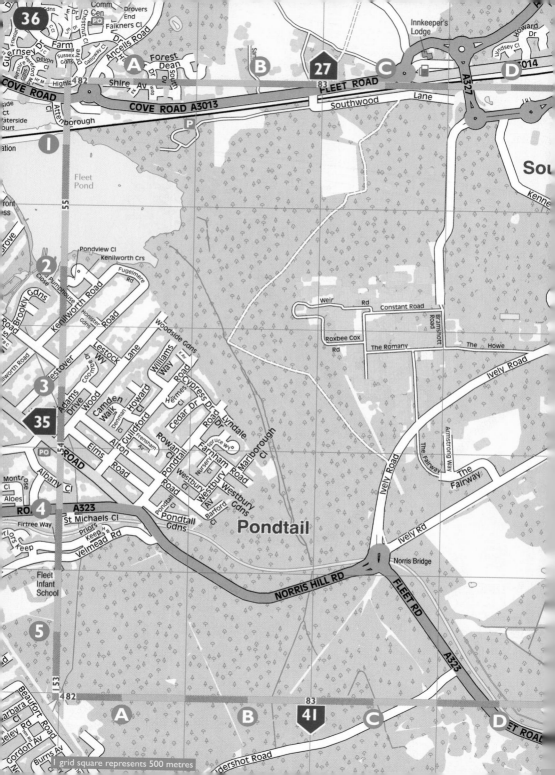

Rafborough

Farnborough Airport

Golf Course

Southwood Golf Club

Travel Inn

Primary School

Arrow Industrial Est

Farnborough Business Centre

Eelmoor Road Trading Est

Eelmoor Road Depot

Farnborough Aerospace Centre

Business Aviation Centre

Aerospace Bvd

Watts Common

Army Golf Club

Golf Course

Kenneis Lane

Ively Road

Ively Road

SUMMIT AVENUE

IVELY RD

IVELY ROAD

ELLES ROAD A327

A327

Southwood

Southern Road

Wisley Gdns

Tarn

Broadmead

Range Rd

Dump Rd

Whitley Way

Rocket Rd

Reservoir Rd

Radar Road

Brake Rd

Tunnel Rd

Cross Rd

Romney Rd

York Road

York Road

Meadow Ga Av

Templer Rd

Perring Rd

Range Road

Boundary Road

Donlan Dr

Vulcan Way

Victor Way

Warwick Rd

Magazine Rd

Wellesley Rd

Windsor Rd

Wapiti Way

Walrus Way

Valiant Way

Wigan Rd

Diamond Way

Vampire Way

Spitfire Way

Swordfish Way

Hurricane Way

Canberra Way

Devon Way

Hinaidi Way

Camel Way

Beaufighter Rd

Gulley Way

Gladiator Way

Aerospace Bvd

Woodside Rd

Shoe Lane

Wellington Way

Stirling Way

Victoria Road

Track

Berkshire Corpse Rd

Sidestrand Wy

Seafire Way

Watts Common Track

Devon Road

Halifax Way

Pavilion

Laffan Road

Eelmoor Bridge

Basingstoke Canal

Columbus Dr

Jubilee Close

Chiltern Cl

Chiltern Avenue

Apollo

Armstrong Mall

Aldri Place

Rise

Southwood Road

Morval Cl

Guttermere Cl

Surgery

Cove CC

Sheffield Cl PO

Welbeck Avenue

Marrowbrook Cl

Cove Road

Tower Hi

Ambleside Cl

Grasmere Rd

Coniston

Ullswater Cl

Rose Gdns

Alpine

Rockey

The Shrubbery

The Lawns

The Topiary

Gleneagles Dr

Long Beech Dr

Laurel Cl

Merlin Way

Delville Cl

Crerar Cl

The Copse

New Dawn

Clifton Cl

Maxwell

Richmond

Pl Cl

Links

Fox Heath

Randolph Dr

McNaught Cl

Summit Av

Larch Way

Wht Gdn

Southwood

Superstore

Surgery

Hazel Dene Rd

Hunter Rd

Halifax Rd

Alison Cl

Busk Crs

Brookhouse

Cody Road

Beverley Crs

Hazel Avenue

Brook Gardens

Kempton Ct

Eelmoor Rd

Arrow Road

Goodden Crs

Keith Lucas Rd

Marrowbrook

Fowler Rd

Montgomery

Murray Av

Weir Rd

Invin

Fowler Av

Ively Road

Range

Link Road

85

86

85

86

E F 28 G H

I

2

3

38

4

5

E F 42 G H

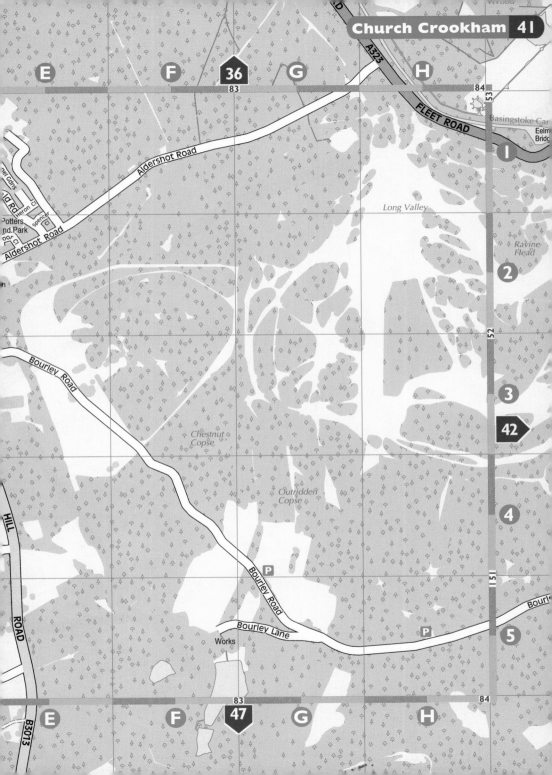

E   F   **36**   G   H

83

84

53

FLEET ROAD

A323

Aldershot Road

Basingstoke Car

Eelm
Brid

I

Long Valley

Ravine
Head

2

Potters
nd.Park

Heron Cl

spencer
Cl

Aldershot Road

ard Rd

52

Bourley Road

3

42

Chestnut
Copse

4

Outridden
Copse

HILL

51

P

Bourley Road

Bourl

ROAD

Bourley Lane

P

5

Works

B3013

83

84

E   F   **47**   G   H

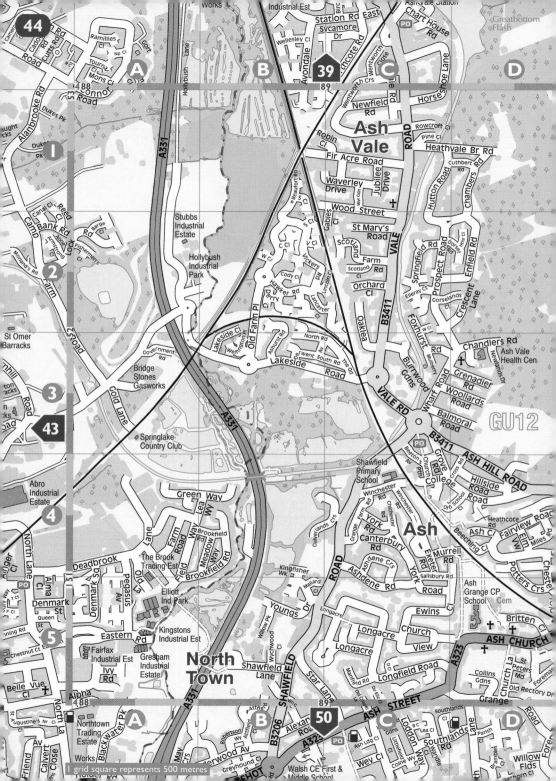

E   F   G   H

91   92

53

I

Ash Common

Wyke Common

2

A324

PIRBRIGHT ROAD

52

3

School Lane

Wyke CP School

Wyke

✝

4

Walden Cottages

Westwood Lane

GUILDFORD ROAD

rackendene

Upr Pinewood Road

Nightingale Rd

Pinewood Rd

Kirriemuir Gdns

X Hills Lane

Ashbourne Close

Ravenscroft Close

A323

PO

Dene Cl

Wyke Avenue

Wyke Lane

51

5 Westwood Place

Harper's

East Wyke Farm

tation

E   F   G   H

91   92

51

Ash Green Road

Road

Jund Fa

E   F   **45**   G   H
91
92

Station

Harper's

East
Wyke Farm

Lane

Road

Ash Green Road

Pound Farm Lane

I

Beech

Drovers
Way

White Lane

Ash

50

Ash   Green   La East

Pound Farm   Green Lane West

2

Farm WK   Old Cross   Tree WY
Pilgrims
Vw

**Ash
Green**

Hazel   Road

Wanbo
Wood

3

White Lane

49

Wyle Road

4

White
Lane Farm

Inwood Farm

Hog's   Back

5

148

E   F   **57**   G   H
91
92

Puttenham   Road

Seale Lane

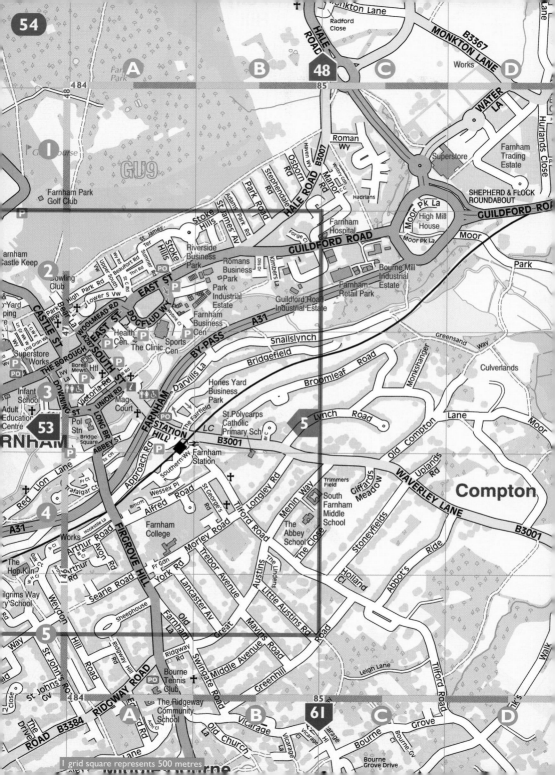

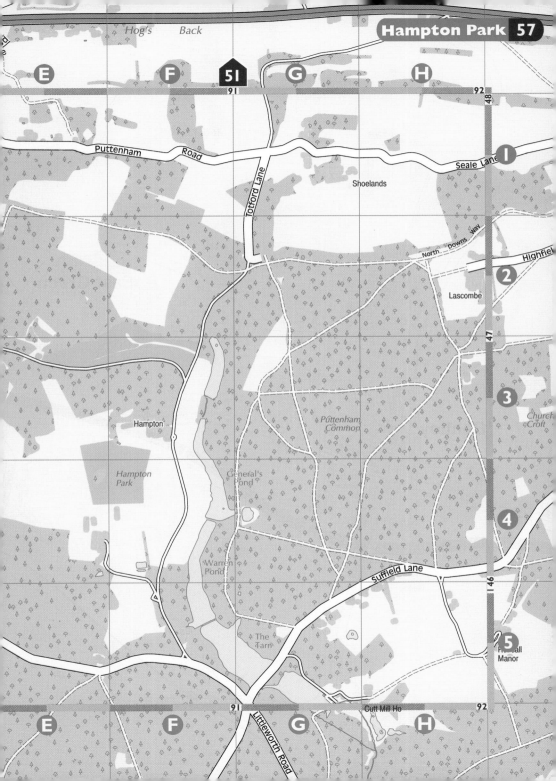

A · B · C · D

478 · 79

1

Bury Court

45

Perryland

2

Church Lane

East Green

Hole Lane

Lane

School

Marsh House

Jenkyn Place

3

Hill

Longcroft

Hole

Eggars Fld

Babs Flds

Lane

Bentley

44

Bonners Fld

Swings Ct

Bus Park

PO

A31

Oakway

Bentley Industrial Cen

Rectory Lane

Park Hill

4

Works

Station Road

Bentley Green Farm

5

143

Wey Bank

Bentley Station

478 · 79

A · B · C · D

Isington Road

Station Road

Gravel Hill

Isington

I grid square represents 500 metres

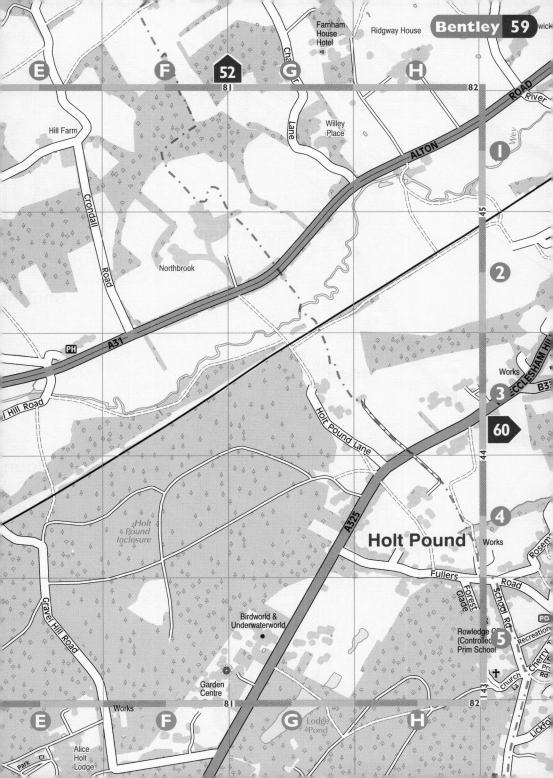

Edgeborough School

E   F   **61**   G   H

85

86

43

I

Kennel Farm

Hill

Kennel La

Fifield Lane

Lane

2

The Reeds Road

Old Frensham Road

Hamlash Lane

Sandy Lane

PO

Millbridge

Shortfield   Road

River Wey (South Branch)

42

Pierreponte School

Priory Lane

3

A287

Frensham Little Pond

The Street

St Marys CE Aided Infant School

Lane End

4

Lovers La

Peakfield

41

ham

Frensham Common Country Park

5

85   86

Bacon

E   F   G   H

Lowicks House

Frensham Great Pond

Aldershot	3 F3	
Ash	44 C4	
Ash Green	51 F2	
Ash Vale	44 C1	
Badshot Lea	49 G4	
Bagshot	8 A5	
Bagshot Heath	15 G2	
Bentley	58 A3	
Bisley	25 H5	
Blackwater	80 B2	
Boundstone	60 D4	
The Bourne	61 G2	
Brookwood	33 G2	
Camberley	14 A4	
Church Crookham	40 B2	
College Town	12 C2	
Compton	54 D4	
Cove	28 C3	
Crawley Hill	22 A1	
Cricket Hill	19 E1	
Crowthorne	6 A3	
Darby Green	11 G5	
Deepcut	31 E3	
Dippenhall	52 D3	
Dockenfield	62 B5	
Donkey Town	16 D5	
Dora's Green	46 C5	
East Green	58 C2	
Elvetham Heath	26 A5	
Ewshot	46 C2	
Farnborough	29 E5	
Farnborough Green	29 G4	
Farnborough Park	38 D1	
Farnborough Street	29 G4	
Fleet	35 G3	
Folly Hill	47 G5	
Fox Lane	20 D5	
Frensham	62 D4	
Frimley	21 G5	
Frimley Green	30 B2	
Frimley Ridge	22 C3	
Frogmore	11 H5	
Hale	48 B5	
Hatton Hill	9 H2	
Hawley	20 C3	
Hawley Lane	29 F2	
Heath End	48 B3	
Heatherside	23 E2	
High Curley	15 F3	
Hog Hatch	47 F4	
Holt Pound	59 H4	
Lane End	63 F4	
Lightwater	16 C5	
Little Sandhurst	11 G1	
Lower Bourne	61 G2	
Lucas Green	24 D2	
Middle Bourne	61 E1	
Millbridge	63 F2	
Montgomery Lines	43 G3	
Moor Park	55 F4	
Mytchett	39 E1	
Mytchett Place	39 H2	
North Camp	43 F1	
North Town	44 A5	
Owlsmoor	12 B1	
Pirbright	33 F5	
Pondtail	36 B4	
Rafborough	37 G1	
Ravenswood Village		
Settlement	6 A1	
Rowledge	60 B5	
Runfold	55 G2	
Sandhurst	11 H2	
The Sands	56 A3	
Sandy Cross	56 B1	
Seale	56 D1	
Sheets Heath	33 F1	
Shortfield Common	62 D1	
Shortheath	60 D2	
South Farnborough	3	
Southwood	3	
Spreakley	6	
Tongham	5	
Upper Hale	4	
Warren Corner	4	
West End	2	
West End	4	
West Heath	5	
Weybourne	5	
Wimble Hill	5	
Windlesham	4	
Wrecclesham	6	
Wyke	4	
Yateley	1	
York Town	2	

USING THE STREET INDEX

Street names are listed alphabetically. Each street name is followed by its postal town or area locality, the Postcode District, the page number, and the reference to the square in which the name is found.

Standard index entries are shown as follows:

Abbetts La *CBLY* GU15 ....**21** F3

Street names and selected addresses not shown on the map due to scale restrictions are shown in the index with an asterisk:

Abbeywood *ASHV* GU12 *.............**44** D3

GENERAL ABBREVIATIONS

ACC	ACCESS	CTYD	COURTYARD	HLS	HILLS	MWY	MOTORWAY	SE	SOUTH
ALY	ALLEY	CUTT	CUTTINGS	HO	HOUSE	N	NORTH	SER	SERVICE A
AP	APPROACH	CV	COVE	HOL	HOLLOW	NE	NORTH EAST	SH	SH
AR	ARCADE	CYN	CANYON	HOSP	HOSPITAL	NW	NORTH WEST	SHOP	SHOP
ASS	ASSOCIATION	DEPT	DEPARTMENT	HRB	HARBOUR	O/P	OVERPASS	SKWY	SKY
AV	AVENUE	DL	DALE	HTH	HEATH	OFF	OFFICE	SMT	SUM
BCH	BEACH	DM	DAM	HTS	HEIGHTS	ORCH	ORCHARD	SOC	SOC
BLDS	BUILDINGS	DR	DRIVE	HVN	HAVEN	OV	OVAL	SP	SP
BND	BEND	DRO	DROVE	HWY	HIGHWAY	PAL	PALACE	SPR	SPR
BNK	BANK	DRY	DRIVEWAY	IMP	IMPERIAL	PAS	PASSAGE	SQ	SQ
BR	BRIDGE	DWGS	DWELLINGS	IN	INLET	PAV	PAVILION	ST	ST
BRK	BROOK	E	EAST	IND EST	INDUSTRIAL ESTATE	PDE	PARADE	STN	STA
BTM	BOTTOM	EMB	EMBANKMENT	INF	INFIRMARY	PH	PUBLIC HOUSE	STR	STR
BUS	BUSINESS	EMBY	EMBASSY	INFO	INFORMATION	PK	PARK	STRD	STR
BVD	BOULEVARD	ESP	ESPLANADE	INT	INTERCHANGE	PKWY	PARKWAY	SW	SOUTH V
BY	BYPASS	EST	ESTATE	IS	ISLAND	PL	PLACE	TDG	TRA
CATH	CATHEDRAL	EX	EXCHANGE	JCT	JUNCTION	PLN	PLAIN	TER	TER
CEM	CEMETERY	EXPY	EXPRESSWAY	JTY	JETTY	PLNS	PLAINS	THWY	THROUGH
CEN	CENTRE	EXT	EXTENSION	KG	KING	PLZ	PLAZA	TNL	TUI
CFT	CROFT	F/O	FLYOVER	KNL	KNOLL	POL	POLICE STATION	TOLL	TOLL
CH	CHURCH	FC	FOOTBALL CLUB	L	LAKE	PR	PRINCE	TPK	TURN
CHA	CHASE	FK	FORK	LA	LANE	PREC	PRECINCT	TR	TF
CHYD	CHURCHYARD	FLD	FIELD	LDG	LODGE	PREP	PREPARATORY	TRL	T
CIR	CIRCLE	FLDS	FIELDS	LGT	LIGHT	PRIM	PRIMARY	TWR	TO
CIRC	CIRCUS	FLS	FALLS	LK	LOCK	PROM	PROMENADE	U/P	UNDER
CL	CLOSE	FLTS	FLATS	LKS	LOCKS	PRS	PRINCESS	UNI	UNIVER
CLFS	CLIFFS	FM	FARM	LNDG	LANDING	PRT	PORT	UPR	UF
CMP	CAMP	FT	FORT	LTL	LITTLE	PT	POINT	V	V
CNR	CORNER	FWY	FREEWAY	LWR	LOWER	PTH	PATH	VA	VA
CO	COUNTY	FY	FERRY	MAG	MAGISTRATE	PZ	PIAZZA	VIAD	VIAL
COLL	COLLEGE	GA	GATE	MAN	MANSIONS	QD	QUADRANT	VIL	V
COM	COMMON	GAL	GALLERY	MD	MEAD	QU	QUEEN	VIS	V
COMM	COMMISSION	GDN	GARDEN	MDW	MEADOWS	QY	QUAY	VLG	VIL
CON	CONVENT	GDNS	GARDENS	MEM	MEMORIAL	R	RIVER	VLS	VI
COT	COTTAGE	GLD	GLADE	MKT	MARKET	RBT	ROUNDABOUT	VW	V
COTS	COTTAGES	GLN	GLEN	MKTS	MARKETS	RD	ROAD	W	W
CP	CAPE	GN	GREEN	ML	MALL	RDG	RIDGE	WD	W
CPS	COPSE	GND	GROUND	ML	MILL	REP	REPUBLIC	WHF	WH
CR	CREEK	GRA	GRANGE	MNR	MANOR	RES	RESERVOIR	WK	W
CREM	CREMATORIUM	GRG	GARAGE	MS	MEWS	RFC	RUGBY FOOTBALL CLUB	WKS	W
CRS	CRESCENT	GT	GREAT	MSN	MISSION	RI	RISE	WLS	W
CSWY	CAUSEWAY	GTWY	GATEWAY	MT	MOUNT	RP	RAMP	WY	W
CT	COURT	GV	GROVE	MTN	MOUNTAIN	RW	ROW	YD	Y
CTRL	CENTRAL	HGR	HIGHER	MTS	MOUNTAINS	S	SOUTH	YHA	YOUTH HO
CTS	COURTS	HL	HILL	MUS	MUSEUM	SCH	SCHOOL		

POSTCODE TOWNS AND AREA ABBREVIATIONS

ALDT	Aldershot	BLKW	Blackwater	FARN	Farnborough	HTWY	Hartley Wintney	SHST	Sandh
ALTN	Alton	CBLY	Camberley	FLEETN	Fleet north	LTWR	Lightwater	WOKN/KNAP	Woking north/Kna
ASHV	Ash Vale	CHOB/PIR	Chobham/Pirbright	FLEETS	Fleet south	MFD/CHID	Milford/Chiddingfold	WOKS/MYFD	Woking so
BAGS	Bagshot	CWTH	Crowthorne	FNM	Farnham	RFNM	Rural Farnham		May
BFOR	Bracknell Forest/Windlesham	EWKG	Wokingham east	FRIM	Frimley	RGUW	Rural Guildford west	YTLY	Yar

Abbetts La *CBLY* GU15	21 F3
Abbey St *FNM* GU9	5 G5
Abbey Wy *FARN* GU14	29 G5
Abbeywood *ASHV* GU12 *	44 D3
Abbots CI *FLEETN* GU51	35 G3
Abbot's Ride *FNM* GU9	4 C5
Abelia CI *CHOB/PIR* GU24	17 E5
Abingdon Rd *SHST* GU47	12 A3
Acacia Av *SHST* GU47	12 B2
Academy CI *CBLY* GU15	14 A3
Academy PI *SHST* GU47	12 A4
Acer Dr *CHOB/PIR* GU24	17 F5
Acheulian CI *FNM* GU9	61 E1
Ackrells Md *SHST* GU47	11 F2
Acorn Keep *FNM* GU9	48 B2
Acorn Rd *BLKW* GU17	19 H1
Adams Cft *CHOB/PIR* GU24	32 C2
Adams Dr *FLEETN* GU51	35 H3
Adams Park Rd *FNM* GU9	54 B1
Addiscombe Rd *CWTH* RG45	7 E4
Addison Rd *FNM* GU16	30 A1
Adlington PI *FARN* GU14	39 E2
Admiralty Wy *CBLY* GU15	20 D2
Aerospace Bvd *ALDT* GU11	38 A5
FARN GU14	37 H5
Ainger CI *ASHV* GU12	3 J1
Aircraft Esp *FARN* GU14	38 C3
Aisne Rd *FRIM* GU16	23 G5
Alamein Rd *ALDT* GU11	2 E2
Albain PI *FARN* GU14	28 B5
Albany CI *FLEETN* GU51	35 H4
Albany Pk *FRIM* GU16	21 G5
Albany Rd *FLEETN* GU51	35 G4
Albert Rd *ALDT* GU11	3 F3
BAGS GU19	15 G2
CBLY GU15 *	13 G5
CWTH RG45	6 D3
FARN GU14	38 C2
Albert St *FLEETN* GU51	35 F3
Albion Rd *SHST* GU47	11 H4
Alcot CI *CWTH* RG45	6 D4
Alderbrook CI *CWTH* RG45	6 A4
Alder CI *ASHV* GU12	39 G5
Alder Gv *YTLY* GU46	11 G1
Aldershot Rd *ASHV* GU12	50 B1
FLEETN GU51	35 G4
FLEETS GU52	40 B3
The Alders *FNM* GU9	49 E4
Aldrin PI *FARN* GU14	28 B5
Aldwick CI *FNM* GU9	29 E5
Aldworth Gdns *CWTH* RG45	6 C3
Alexandra Av *CBLY* GU15	21 E1
Alexandra Ct *FARN* GU14	38 C3
Alexandra Rd *ALDT* GU11	48 C1
ASHV GU12	50 B1
FARN GU14	38 D3
Alexandra Ter *ALDT* GU11 *	2 C3
Alfonso CI *ASHV* GU12	3 H6
Alfred CI *FLEETN* GU51	34 D1
Alfred Rd *FNM* GU9	5 H5
Alfriston Rd *FRIM* GU16	31 E2
Alice Rd *ALDT* GU11	2 E3
Alison CI *FARN* GU14	37 H1
Alington Gn *FRIM* GU16	22 B1
Alison's Rd *ALDT* GU11	43 E2
Alison's Rd *ALDT* GU11	2 A3
Allden Av *ASHV* GU12	49 H3
Allden Gdns *ASHV* GU12	49 H3
Allenby Rd *CBLY* GU15	13 E5
Allendale CI *SHST* GU47	11 G1
All Hallows Av *CHOB/PIR* GU24	33 H4
All Saints Crs *FARN* GU14	20 C5
All Saints Rd *LTWR* GU18	1
All Souls Av *CHOB/PIR* GU24	3
Alma CI *ASHV* GU12	
Alma Gdns *FRIM* GU16	3
Alma La *FNM* GU9	4
Alma Wy *FNM* GU9	
Almond CI *FARN* GU14	2
The Aloes *FLEETN* GU51	
Alpha Rd *ASHV* GU12	
Alphington Av *FRIM* GU16	2
Alphington Gn *FRIM* GU16	2
Alpine CI *FARN* GU14	
Alsford CI *LTWR* GU18	
Alton Ride *BLKW* GU17	
Alton Rd *FLEETN* GU51	3
RFNM GU10	
Alverstoke Gdns *ALDT* GU11	3
Alwin PI *FNM* GU9	
Ambarrow Crs *SHST* GU47	

rrow La CWTH RG45 .....10 D1
m CBLY GU15 ....22 D2
rley Gra ALDT GU11 ....2 A6
wood Dr RFNM GU10 ....14 B4
eside CI FARN GU14 ....28 C5
M GU10 ....39 C2
side Crs FNM GU9 .....47 C4
eside Rd LTWR GU18 ...16 A3
s Rd FLEETN GU51 .....28 A5
er Meadow FARN GU14 ..28 D5
son PI BAGS GU19 .....8 C4
ver Ter Rd BLKW GU17 ..12 A5
ver Wy ALDT GU11 .....49 F3
wartha Rd FARN GU14 ..39 E3
ers CI FLEETS GU52 ....40 C1
sev Av FARN GU14 .....28 C4
sey Rd ASHV GU12 .....3 J4
a Wy FLEETN GU51 .....26 D5
ndale Dr RFNM GU10 ...61 F2
Armstrong CI
OT GU11 ....43 H2
wy FLEETS GU52 ....40 D1
tes Cft FLEETS GU52 ...40 A3
Rd FNM GU16 ....30 A1
CI ALDT GU11 ....2 A1
Dr FNM GU16 ....2 D2
by LTWR GU18 ....16 A2
RI FARN GU14 ....28 B5
ndore Ms FARN GU14 ...29 E2
lands CI RFNM GU10 ...60 C4
Tree Wy SHST GU47 ....12 B2
Dr CBLY GU15 ....21 F1
each Rd FNM GU9 ......53 G5
scl CBLY GU15 ....21 C4
en Rd YTLY GU46 * 18 C2
rcade ALDT GU11 * 2 C3
ssan Av CBLY GU15 ....22 C2
ell CI CWTH RG45 .....6 B3
La ALDT GU11 ....42 C5
al Dr CWTH RG45 ......6 B1
usa Wy CHOB/PIR GU24 ..25 F3
te CI FLEETN GU51 .....26 D5
at Ter SHST GU47 * 12 C3
te St CHOB/PIR GU24 ...32 A3
ton Ter ALDT GU11 ....2 B5
age Dr FRIM GU16 .....28 D5
trong Mi FARN GU14 ...28 B5
rong Wy FARN GU14 ....36 D3
en CI ALDT GU11 ......2 A1
y Rd FARN GU14 ....37 H2
r Rd BAGS GU19 ....15 C2
M GU9 ....5 F6
r Rd FNM GU9 ....2 E4
st ALDT GU11 ....2 E4
ery Rd ALDT GU11 * 2 E4
OT GU11 ....31 H5
del CI FLEETN GU51 ....35 H4
Wy FARN GU14 ....4 E3
del Rd CBLY GU15 .....40 D1
Ct ALDT GU11 ....2 B5
ourne CI ASHV GU12 ...45 E4
ry Dr FARN GU14 ......21 E5
hurch Rd ASHV GU12 ...44 D1
S ASHV GU12 ....44 D1
..............20 A1
ene Crs ASHV GU12 ....44 C4
ne CI ASHV GU12 ......44 C4
own Av FARN GU14 .....39 E2
eld Gn YTLY GU46 .....19 F1
reen La East ASHV GU12 ..11 K2
reen La West
HV 50 B2
reen Rd ASHV GU12 ....51 E1
ill Rd ASHV GU12 .....50 D4
y CI FRIM GU16 ....30 C3
y Dr BLKW GU17 ....20 A2
y Av FARN GU14 ....29 H5
y Wy CHOB/PIR GU24 ...50 C1
odge CI ASHV GU12 ....50 C1
odge FARN GU14 ....28 D2
d ASHV GU12 ....3 J4
t ASHV GU12 ....44 C5
ree CI FARN GU14 .....37 E1
rst Rd ASHV GU12 .....44 B3
rst Av CBLY GU15 .....14 B5
n Gv ASHV GU12 ....50 A2
y BLKW GU17 ....19 H1
d Gv FLEETS GU52 .....40 C3
d Gv BFOR GU20 ....9 H4
patti Rd SHST GU47 ...12 A2
borough CI FLEETS GU51 ..35 H1
id CI ASHV GU12 ......50 B1
Gdns FLEETS GU52 .....23 E1
inleck Wy ALDT GU11 ..1 J2
stus Gdns FLEETS GU52 ..23 E1
en Rd FARN GU14 ......60 D1
ey La FNM GU9 ....60 D1
ue De Cagny
OB/PIR GU24 ....33 F4
ue Rd FARN GU14 ......29 H5
ue St FLEETS GU52 ....15 F2
ue Sucy CBLY GU15 ....21 E2
Avenue ALDT GU11 ....49 G3
VTH RG45 ....6 E3
WR GU18 ....16 A2
M GU10 ....60 B4
et Crs SHST GU47 .....12 B1
CI ASHV GU12 ....44 C5
RN GU14 ....29 E1
dale ASHV GU12 ......39 F5
dale Rd ALDT GU11 ....3 F6
EETN GU51 ....35 G2
HI GU11 ....2 A5

Ayling La ALDT GU11 ....2 B6
Ayrshire Gdns FLEETN GU51 ..26 D5
Azalea Gdns FLEETS GU52 ..40 D2
Azalea Wy CBLY GU15 ...14 D5

B

Babbs Md FNM GU9 .....4 D5
Babs Flds RFNM GU10 ..58 A3
Back Dr CWTH RG45 * ..6 D5
Bacon CI SHST GU47 ...12 B5
Badajos Rd ALDT GU11 ..2 A1
Badger Dr LTWR GU18 ..16 A2
Badgers CI FLEETS GU52 ..35 F4
Badgers Copse CBLY GU15 ..22 A5
Badgers Holt YTLY GU46 ..18 B1
Badgers Sett CWTH RG45 ..6 B3
Badger Wy RFNM GU10 ..46 D2
Badgerwood Dr FRIM GU16 ..21 H4
Badshot Lea Rd FNM GU9 ..49 F4
Badshot Pk FRIM GU16 ..49 E4
Bagshot Gn BAGS GU19 ..8 C5
Bagshot Rd CHOB/PIR GU24 ..17 H5
  WOKN/KNAP GU21 .....33 H1
Baigents La BFOR GU20 ..9 H4
Bailey CI FRIM GU16 ....29 H1
Baileys CI BLKW GU17 ...19 H2
Bain Av FARN GU14 ....21 F5
Baird Rd FARN GU14 ...29 G5
Bakehouse Gdns FLEETS GU52 ..40 B3
Bakehouse Ms ALDT GU11 * ..2 D2
Baldreys FNM GU9 .....53 G5
Balintore Ct SHST GU47 ..12 B4
Ballantyne Rd FARN GU14 ..29 E5
Ballard Rd CBLY GU15 ..14 C5
Balliard Wy SHST GU47 ..12 C2
Balloon Rd FARN GU14 ..38 B2
Ball & Wicket La FNM GU9 ..48 A5
Balmoral Crs FNM GU9 ..47 H4
Balmoral Dr FRIM GU16 ..30 A1
Balmoral Rd ASHV GU12 ..45 E4
Banbury CI FRIM GU16 ..30 B2
Bank Rd ALDT GU11 ....43 H2
Bankside FNM GU9 .....48 D5
Bannister Gdns YTLY GU46 ..11 H5
Barbara CI FLEETS GU52 ..40 D1
Barberry CI FLEETS GU52 ..40 C1
Barberry Wy BLKW GU17 ..23 F5
Barbon CI CBLY GU15 ...30 B2
Bardsley Dr FNM GU9 ..53 H5
Barford CI FLEETN GU51 ..36 B4
Barge CI ALDT GU11 ...44 A2
Barkis Md SHST GU47 ..12 C1
Barley Wy FLEETS GU52 ..26 D4
Barnard CI FRIM GU16 ..30 B1
Barnard Wy ALDT GU11 ..2 B1
Barn CI CBLY GU15 ....14 A5
Barncroft FNM GU9 ....29 H5
Barnes CI FARN GU14 ..29 H5
Barnes Rd FRIM GU16 ..30 A1
Barnett La LTWR GU18 ..15 H4
Barnfield YTLY GU46 ..18 D1
Barn Meadow Ct FLEETS GU52 ..24 C4
Barnsford Crs CHOB/PIR GU24 ..17 G4
Barnsley CI FRIM GU16 ..39 H3
Barossa Rd CBLY GU15 ..13 H4
Barracane Dr CWTH RG45 ..6 C4
Barrack Rd ALDT GU11 ..3 G6
Barrie Rd FNM GU9 ....47 G3
Bartlett PI FRIM GU16 ..30 B4
Barton CI ALDT GU11 ..48 C1
Barton's Dr YTLY GU46 ..18 D2
Bartons Wy FARN GU14 ..38 A4
Barwell CI CWTH RG45 ..6 B4
Basingstoke CI FLEETS GU52 ..40 C1
Basingbourne CI FLEETS GU52 ..40 D1
Basing Dr ALDT GU11 ..49 F3
Bassett CI FRIM GU16 ..30 A1
Bat and Ball La FARN GU14 ..60 C2
Bath Rd CBLY GU15 ....13 G5
Bayfield Av FRIM GU16 ..22 A1
Bayford CI FARN GU14 ..21 E5
Baywood CI FARN GU14 ..60 C1
Beacon CI RFNM GU10 ..60 C5
Beacon Gdns FLEETS GU51 * ..35 F4
Beacon Hill Rd FLEETS GU52 ..40 D3
  RFNM GU10 ....47 E1
Beacon Rd FARN GU14 ..38 A4
Beales La RFNM GU10 ..60 B1
Bealeswood La RFNM GU10 ..62 A5
Beam Hollow FNM GU9 ..48 A5
Bear La FNM GU9 ......48 B5
Bearwood Gdns FLEETS GU51 ..35 G5
Beaufighter Rd FARN GU14 ..38 A4
Beaufort Rd ASHV GU12 ..44 B2
  FLEETS GU52 ....35 H5
Beaufront CI CBLY GU15 ..14 C4
Beaufront Rd CBLY GU15 ..14 C4
Beaulieu Gdns BLKW GU17 ..20 B1
Beaumaris Pde FRIM GU16 ..30 B1
Beaumonts ALDT GU11 ..42 C5
Beaver La YTLY GU46 ..19 E1
Beavers Hi FNM GU9 ...4 A4
Beavers Rd FNM GU9 ..4 A4
Beck Gdns FARN GU14 ..47 G4
Bedford Av FRIM GU16 ..30 B4
Beds CI FRIM GU16 ....30 A3
Beech Av CBLY GU15 ..21 H2
  FARN GU14 ....61 E3
Beechbrook Av YTLY GU46 ..18 D1
Beech CI ASHV GU12 ..50 A2
Beech Dr BLKW GU17 ..19 H2
The Beeches ASHV GU12 ..39 F3
Beech Gv CHOB/PIR GU24 ..32 C2
Beeching CI ASHV GU12 ..44 D4
Beechnut Dr BLKW GU17 ..11 H5
Beechnut Rd ASHV GU12 ..3 F4
Beech Ride FLEETS GU52 ..35 H5
  SHST GU47 ....11 H5

Beech Rd FARN GU14 ..29 F2
  FNM GU16 ....30 B3
Beech Tree Dr FNM GU9 ..49 E5
Beechwood CI FLEETS GU51 ..40 A1
Beeton's Av ASHV GU12 ..44 C5
Beldam Bridge Rd
  CHOB/PIR GU24 ......17 G5
Beldham Rd RFNM GU10 ..60 B1
Belfry Ms SHST GU47 ..11 F3
Belgrave Ct BLKW GU17 ..20 B5
Belland Dr ALDT GU11 ..48 C1
Bell CI FARN GU14 ....29 G5
Believer HI CBLY GU15 ..3 K3
Belle Vue Ct ASHV GU12 ..3 J3
Bellew Rd FRIM GU16 ..30 D5
Bellingham Ct CBLY GU15 ..23 E2
Bell La BLKW GU17 ....20 A1
Bell PI BAGS GU19 ....8 D5
Belmont Ct FARN GU14 ..28 D2
Belmont Ms CBLY GU15 ..21 G3
Belmont Rd CBLY GU15 ..21 G2
  CWTH RG45 ....6 D5
Belsize Rd FARN GU14 ..38 C3
Belstone Ms FARN GU14 ..29 E2
Belton Rd CBLY GU15 ..22 A1
Belvedere CI FLEETN GU51 ..34 C5
Belvedere CI BLKW GU17 ..20 B1
Belvedere Rd FARN GU14 ..38 C2
Belvoir CI FRIM GU16 ..22 B5
Bembridge Ct CWTH RG45 ..6 B4
Bencteng CI FLEETN GU51 ..34 C5
Benner La CHOB/PIR GU24 ..17 F4
Bennett Ct FARN GU14 ..21 C1
Bennetts Ri ALDT GU11 ..3 G7
Benson Rd CWTH RG45 ..6 B5
Bentley Copse CBLY GU15 ..22 D2
Ben Well Rd CHOB/PIR GU24 ..33 F2
Benwell Rd FARN GU14 ..33 C1
Beresford Ct FRIM GU16 ..30 B3
Bergenia Ct CHOB/PIR GU24 ..17 E5
Berkeley CI FLEETN GU51 ..35 H5
Berkeley Crs FRIM GU16 ..30 C1
Berkshire Corpse Rd
  ALDT GU11 ....37 C5
Berkshire Rd CBLY GU15 ..14 B3
Bermersh CI SHST GU47 ..12 C2
Berrybank SHST GU47 ..12 C5
Beta Rd FARN GU14 ...28 D4
Bethel CI FNM GU9 ....48 B4
Bethel La FNM GU9 ....48 B4
Betjeman Wk YTLY GU46 ..11 F3
Beveren CI FLEETN GU51 ..26 D5
Beverley CI FARN GU14 ..50 B1
  RFNM GU10 ....60 C4
Beverley CI CBLY GU15 ..15 E5
Beverley Crs FARN GU14 ..37 H1
Bicknell Rd FRIM GU16 ..22 A4
Bideford Ct FARN GU14 ..37 H1
Bildesden Rd CHOB/PIR GU24 ..32 C5
Binsted Dr BLKW GU17 ..20 B1
Binton La RFNM GU10 ..56 A5
Birch Av FLEETN GU51 ..35 F3
Birch CI CBLY GU15 ...14 C5
  RFNM GU10 ....60 C4
Birch Dr BLKW GU17 ..20 B5
The Birches BLKW GU17 ..19 H1
  FARN GU14 ....28 B5
Birchett Rd ALDT GU11 ..2 C4
  FARN GU14 ....28 C4
Birchfields CBLY GU15 ..39 G2
Birch La CHOB/PIR GU24 ..16 D4
Birch Platt CHOB/PIR GU24 ..16 D5
Birch Side CWTH RG45 ..6 B2
Birch Tree Vw LTWR GU18 ..16 A2
Birchview CI YTLY GU46 ..18 C2
Birch Wy ASHV GU12 ..39 G5
Birchwood Dr LTWR GU18 ..16 C2
Birdhaven RFNM GU10 ..60 C3
Birds Gv WOKN/KNAP GU21 ..25 H5
Birdwood Rd CBLY GU15 ..13 G5
Birkbeck PI SHST GU47 ..12 C1
Bishops CI FLEETS GU52 ..35 G5
Bishops Gv BFOR GU20 ..9 G4
Bishop's Md FNM GU9 ..4 B3
Bishop's Wy ALDT GU11 ..47 H4
Bishop Sumner Dr FNM GU9 ..48 A4
Bittern CI ALDT GU11 ..49 E3
  SHST GU47 ....12 B5
Blackbird CI SHST GU47 ..12 B5
Blackbullie Pk YTLY GU46 * ..18 C1
Blackbushes Rd FLEETN GU51 ..26 A5
Blackcap PI SHST GU47 ..12 C2
Blackdown CI FRIM GU16 ..31 D2
Blackheath Rd FNM GU9 ..47 G5
Blackman Gdns ALDT GU11 ..3 F7
Blacke Pond La RFNM GU10 ..61 E2
Blackstone Ct FARN GU14 ..28 B3
Blackstroud La East
  LTWR GU18 ....16 D3
Blackstroud La West
  LTWR GU18 ....16 D3
Blackthorn Crs FARN GU14 ..28 D1
Blackthorn Dr LTWR GU18 ..16 B4
Blackwater CI ASHV GU12 ..50 C1
Blackwater Pk ASHV GU12 ..50 A1
Blackwater Vw EWKG RG40 ..10 A1
Blackwater Wy ASHV GU12 ..3 K7
Blaire Pk YTLY GU46 ..11 G4
Blaise CI FARN GU14 ..38 D1
Blake CI CWTH RG45 ..7 E4
Blakes Ride YTLY GU46 ..10 B5
Blenheim CI RFNM GU10 ..60 B3
Blenheim Ct FARN GU14 ..38 D2
Blenheim Rd ALDT GU11 ..38 C5
Blenheim Pk ALDT GU11 ..38 C5
Blenheim Rd ALDT GU11 ..38 C5
Bligton La RFNM GU10 ..57 H3
Bloomsbury Wy BLKW GU17 ..23 G5
Bluebell PI FARN GU14 ..28 D1
Blue Prior CI FLEETS GU52 ..40 A4
Bluethroat CI SHST GU47 ..12 C3
Bluff Cove ALDT GU11 ..3 H1
Blunden Rd FARN GU14 ..28 D4
Blythwood Dr FRIM GU16 ..21 H4

Bofors Rd FARN GU14 ..38 A4
Bolding House La
  CHOB/PIR GU24 ......17 F5
Bonners Fld FLEETN GU51 ..58 A3
Borderside YTLY GU46 ..10 A5
Borelli Ms FNM GU9 ...5 G5
The Borough FNM GU9 ..5 G5
Bosman Dr BFOR GU20 ..9 F1
Botany HI RFNM GU10 ..55 H4
Boulevards ALDT GU11 * ..2 D3
Boulters Rd ASHV GU12 ..3 H4
Boundary Rd FARN GU14 ..37 E3
  FARN GU14 ....38 C2
  RFNM GU10 ....62 A4
Boundstone CI RFNM GU10 ..60 D5
Boundstone Rd RFNM GU10 ..60 B4
Bourley La RFNM GU10 ..60 D5
Bourley Rd FLEETS GU52 ..41 E5
Bourne CI ALDT GU11 ..2 C6
Bourne Dene RFNM GU10 ..60 C3
Bourne Firs RFNM GU10 ..61 F3
Bourne Gv FNM GU10 ..61 G1
Bourne Grove CI FNM GU9 ..61 G1
Bourne Grove Dr RFNM GU10 ..61 G1
Bourne Hts FNM GU9 * ..54 A5
The Bourne FLEETS GU52 ..40 C1
Bowenhurst Gdns
  FLEETS GU52 ....40 C3
Bowenhurst La FLEETS GU52 ..40 C4
Bower Rd RFNM GU10 ..60 C3
Bowling Court Gn FNM GU9 ..30 A2
Bowman Ct CWTH RG45 ..6 A4
Boxall's Gv ALDT GU11 ..2 C7
Boxall's La ALDT GU11 ..49 E5
  FNM GU9 ....2 B7
Boxhalls La ALDT GU11 ..2 B7
Brabon Rd FARN GU14 ..28 D4
Bracebridge CBLY GU15 ..21 E1
Brackendale CI FRIM GU16 ..22 A5
Brackendale Rd CBLY GU15 ..21 H2
Brackenden ASHV GU12 ..45 E4
Bracken La YTLY GU46 ..10 B5
The Brackens CWTH RG45 ..6 C1
Brackenwood CBLY GU15 ..23 F1
Bracklesham CI FARN GU14 ..29 E2
Bracknell CI FRIM GU16 ..22 B2
Bracknell Rd BAGS GU19 ..8 C1
  CWTH RG45 ....7 F2
Braemar CI FRIM GU16 ..30 B1
Brake Rd FARN GU14 ..37 G3
Bramble Bank FRIM GU16 ..30 C5
Bramblegate CWTH RG45 ..6 C2
Brambles CI ALDT GU11 * ..50 D1
Brambleton Av FNM GU9 ..60 D1
Bramblewood PI FLEETN GU51 ..35 F5
Bramcote CBLY GU15 ..23 E1
Bramley La BLKW GU17 ..19 H1
Bramley Rd CBLY GU15 ..21 F4
Bramling Av YTLY GU46 ..10 B5
Bramshot Dr FLEETN GU51 ..35 G2
Bramshot La FARN GU14 ..28 A3
  FLEETN GU51 ....27 G4
Bramshott Rd FARN GU14 ..36 C2
Brandon Ct CBLY GU15 ..23 F2
Brandon Rd FLEETS GU52 ..40 A3
Brandy Bottom BLKW GU17 * ..19 E3
Branksome CI ASHV GU12 ..14 A5
Branksome Hill Rd SHST GU47 ..12 C4
Branksome Park Rd
  CBLY GU15 ....14 A5
Branksomewood Rd
  FLEETN GU51 ....35 E3
Braye CI SHST GU47 ..12 C4
Brecon CI FARN GU14 ..28 B2
The Breech CBLY GU15 ..12 C4
Brendon Rd FARN GU14 ..28 B2
Brentmoor Rd CHOB/PIR GU24 ..16 C5
Bret Harte Rd FRIM GU16 ..22 A5
Brewers Ct FARN GU14 ..37 H1
Briar Av LTWR GU18 ..15 H4
Briars Ct FARN GU14 ..37 F1
The Briars RFNM GU10 ..50 D1
  FLEETS GU52 ....40 C1
Brick La FLEETN GU51 ..35 G2
Bricksbury HI FNM GU9 ..47 H3
Bridge End CBLY GU15 ..21 F2
Bridgefield FNM GU9 ..5 J3
Bridgemead FRIM GU16 ..29 H1
Bridge Rd ALDT GU11 ..2 D6
  BAGS GU19 ....8 C5
  CBLY GU15 ....21 F3
  FARN GU14 ....28 D5
Bridge Sq FNM GU9 ...5 G4
Bridge Wk YTLY GU46 ..10 C4
Brighton Rd ALDT GU11 ..3 H7
Brightwells Rd FARN GU14 ..28 D5
Brindle CI ALDT GU11 ..49 E5
Brinksway FLEETN GU51 ..35 G4
Brinn's La BLKW GU17 ..20 A1
Bristow Rd CBLY GU15 ..21 F5
Britten CI ASHV GU12 ..44 D5
Broadacres FLEETN GU51 ..34 D4
Broad Ha'penny RFNM GU10 ..60 C5
Broadhurst FARN GU14 ..28 A5
Broadlands FARN GU14 ..39 E2
  FNM GU9 ....30 B1
Broadley Gn BFOR GU20 ..9 F1
Broadmead FARN GU14 ..37 F1
Broad St CHOB/PIR GU24 ..16 D4
Broad Wk FARN GU14 ..22 A4
Broad Wy FARN GU14 ..38 A4
Broadway WOKN/KNAP GU21 ..25 H5
Broadway Rd CHOB/PIR GU24 ..16 D1
The Broadway SHST GU47 ..11 H4
Broadwell Rd RFNM GU10 ..60 B2
Brock CI FRIM GU16 ..31 F1
Brockenhurst Dr YTLY GU46 ..18 B1
Brockenhurst Rd ALDT GU11 ..2 E6
Brockhurst Ldg FNM GU9 ..60 D1
Brocklands YTLY GU46 ..18 B2
Brokie CI FLEETS GU52 ..40 A3
Brook Av FNM GU9 ....48 D5
Brook CI FLEETN GU51 ..15 G4
  SHST GU47 ....13 C2

Brookers Cnr CWTH RG45 ..7 E3
Brookers Rw CWTH RG45 ..7 E2
Brookfield Rd ASHV GU12 ..44 A5
Brook Gdns FARN GU14 ..37 H2
Brookhouse Rd FARN GU14 ..37 H1
Brooklands CI FNM GU9 ..48 B3
  RFNM GU10 ....58 B3
Brooklands Rd FNM GU9 ..48 B3
Brooklands Wy FNM GU9 ..48 C3
Brookley CI RFNM GU10 ..55 F2
Brookly Gdns FLEETN GU51 ..35 H5
Brookmead Ct FNM GU9 ..5 G6
Brook Rd BAGS GU19 ..15 C1
  CBLY GU15 ....21 H2
Brooksby CI BLKW GU17 ..19 H1
Brookside FNM GU9 ....48 A4
  SHST GU47 ....12 A4
Brookside Pk FARN GU14 * ..21 E5
Brookwood Br
  WOKN/KNAP GU21 .....33 H2
Brookwood Lye Rd
  WOKN/MYFD GU22 ....33 H2
Brookwood Rd FARN GU14 ..29 H5
  SHST GU47 ....11 H5
Broome CI YTLY GU46 ..10 C4
Broom Fld LTWR GU18 ..16 A2
Broomfield La ALDT GU11 ..62 C2
Broomhill RFNM GU10 ..46 D2
Broomhill Rd FARN GU14 ..28 B4
Broomleaf Cnr FNM GU9 ..5 K4
Broomleaf Rd FNM GU9 ..5 K5
Broomrigg Rd FLEETN GU51 ..34 D2
Broomsquires Rd BAGS GU19 ..15 C1
Broom Wy BLKW GU17 ..20 B2
Broomwood Wy RFNM GU10 ..61 E2
Brougham PI FNM GU9 ..47 H5
Broughton Ms FRIM GU16 ..22 B5
Browning CI CBLY GU15 ..23 E2
Browning Rd FLEETS GU52 ..40 A4
Brownsover Rd FARN GU14 ..28 A5
Browns Wk RFNM GU10 ..60 B3
Brunswick CHOB/PIR GU24 ..32 D2
Brunswick Rd CHOB/PIR GU24 ..32 A4
  FRIM GU16 ....31 F3
Bruntile CI FARN GU14 ..38 D3
Bryanstone CI FLEETS GU52 ..40 C1
Bryce Gdns ALDT GU11 ..49 C5
Bryn Rd RFNM GU10 ...60 B1
The Buchan CBLY GU15 ..14 C3
Buckhurst Rd FRIM GU16 ..30 B3
Buckland CI FARN GU14 ..29 G2
Buckingham Wy FRIM GU16 ..30 B1
Buller Ct FARN GU14 ..38 C3
Buller Rd FARN GU14 ..43 F3
Bullers Rd FNM GU9 ..4 C5
Bullfinch CI SHST GU47 ..12 C5
Bungalow Rd FARN GU14 ..38 B2
Burbury Woods CBLY GU15 ..14 A5
Burdock CI LTWR GU18 ..16 B3
Burford Rd CBLY GU15 ..21 F2
Burghead CI SHST GU47 ..12 B4
Burgoyne Rd CBLY GU15 ..14 C5
Burleigh Rd FRIM GU16 ..29 H1
Burley Wy BLKW GU17 ..12 A5
Burlington Ct ALDT GU11 ..2 B5
  BLKW GU17 ....20 A3
Burne-Jones Dr SHST GU47 ..12 B5
Burnet CI CHOB/PIR GU24 ..17 E5
Burnham CI FARN GU14 ..29 F5
Burnsall CI FARN GU14 ..28 D3
Burns Av FLEETS GU52 ..40 D1
Burns CI FARN GU14 ..28 D3
Burnside FLEETN GU51 ..35 C4
Burnt Hill Rd RFNM GU10 ..60 C2
Burnt Hill Wy RFNM GU10 ..60 D5
Burnt Pollard La
  CHOB/PIR GU24 ......17 C2
Burrell Rd FRIM GU16 ..30 B3
Burwood Gdns ASHV GU12 ..44 C3
Bury Rd FARN GU14 ..37 H1
Butler End BAGS GU19 ..15 H1
  CWTH RG45 ....6 D2
Butterfield CBLY GU15 ..21 F2
Buttermere CI RFNM GU10 ..60 A1
Buttermere CI FARN GU14 ..28 C5
Buttermere Ct ASHV GU12 * ..44 B5
Buttermere Dr CBLY GU15 ..23 F2
Byron Av FRIM GU16 ..22 D5
Byron CI FLEETS GU52 ..35 G4
  YTLY GU46 ....18 B2
Byron Dr CWTH RG45 ..6 D5
Byways YTLY GU46 ...18 B1
Byworth CI FNM GU9 ..4 B3
Byworth Rd FNM GU9 ..4 B4

C

Cabrol Rd FARN GU14 ..29 E4
Cadet Wy FLEETS GU52 ..40 D3
Cadnam CI ALDT GU11 ..49 G4
Cadogan Rd ALDT GU11 ..38 D5
Caernarvon FRIM GU16 ..30 B1
Caesar's Camp Rd CBLY GU15 ..14 C3
Caesar's CI CBLY GU15 ..14 D3
Cairn CI FRIM GU16 ..22 D5
Cairngorm PI FARN GU14 ..28 C2
Calcott Pk YTLY GU46 ..10 C5
Caldwell Rd BFOR GU20 ..9 H3
Caledonia Rd ASHV GU12 ..3 K4
Calthorpe Rd FLEETN GU51 ..35 E2
Calton Gdns ALDT GU11 ..49 G5
Calvert CI ASHV GU12 ..3 K5
Calvin CI CBLY GU15 ..22 D2
Cambrian CI CBLY GU15 ..21 F1
Cambrian Rd FARN GU14 ..28 B2
Cambridge Rd ALDT GU11 ..2 A3
  CWTH RG45 ....7 E4
  SHST GU47 ....12 C2
Cambridge Rd East
  FARN GU14 ....38 D3
Cambridge Rd West
  FARN GU14 ....38 C3

Camden Wk FLEETN GU51 ....36 A3
Camellia Ct CHOB/PIR GU24......17 F5
Cam Wy FARN GU14 ....38 A4
Cameron Rd ALDT GU11 ....38 D5
Campbell Cl ALDT GU11 ....49 F3
  FLEETN GU51 ....35 E3
  YTLY GU46 ....11 F5
Campbell Pl FNM GU16 ....22 B5
Campbell Rd ALDT GU11 ....54 C3
Camp Farm Rd ALDT GU11 ....43 H2
Camp Hl RFNM GU10 ....55 G5
Campion Cl BLKW GU17 ....20 D3
Canada Rd FRIM GU16 ....31 F1
Canal Cl ALDT GU11 ....43 H2
Canberra Cl HTWY RG27 ....10 A4
Canberra Wy FARN GU14 ....37 H4
Canning Rd ALDT GU11 ....3 J5
Cannon Cl SHST GU47 ....12 B3
Canterbury Rd ASHV GU12 ....44 C4
  FARN GU14 ....38 D2
Capper Rd CBLY GU15 ....13 E4
The Cardinals RFNM GU10 ....50 B5
Carfax Av RFNM GU10 ....60 B2
Cargate Av ALDT GU11 ....2 C4
Cargate Gv ALDT GU11 ....2 B5
Cargate Hl ALDT GU11 ....2 B4
Cargate Ter ALDT GU11 ....2 C5
Carisbrooke FRIM GU16 ....30 B1
Carlin Pl CBLY GU15 ....21 G2
Carlinwark Dr CBLY GU15 ....14 B4
Carlton Cl FARN GU14 ....22 D3
Carlton Crs FLEETS GU52 ....40 D1
Carlyon Cl FARN GU14 ....29 F5
  FRIM GU16 ....30 B5
Carmarthen Cl FARN GU14 ....28 D2
Caroline Wy FRIM GU16 ....22 B5
Carrick La YTLY GU46 ....11 E5
Carrington La ASHV GU12 ....39 F4
Carshalton Rd CBLY GU15 ....14 C2
Carters Wk FNM GU9 ....48 B2
Carthona Dr FLEETS GU52 ....35 F5
Cassino Cl ALDT GU11 ....2 E2
Castle Cl CBLY GU15 ....22 B2
Castlecraig Ct SHST GU47 * 12 B4
Castle Fld FNM GU9 ....4 E2
Castle Hl FNM GU9 ....4 E2
Castle Rd ALDT GU11 ....42 C3
  CBLY GU15 ....55 F5
Castle St FLEETS GU52 ....55 F5
  FNM GU9 ....5 F2
Castor Ct FLEETS GU52 ....40 D2
  YTLY GU46 ....10 B4
Caswall Ride YTLY GU46 ....19 H1
Caswell Cl FARN GU14 ....28 D3
Catena Ri LTWR GU18 ....16 A2
Caterham Cl CHOB/PIR GU24.....33 E3
Catesby Gdns YTLY GU46 ....18 A1
Cavalry Ct ALDT GU11 ....42 C5
Cavan's Rd ALDT GU11 ....3 J7
Cavendish Cl FARN GU14 ....28 C4
Cavendish Ct BLKW GU17 ....20 B3
Cavendish Gdns FLEETS GU52 ....40 A2
Cavendish Ms ALDT GU11 ....2 C5
Cavendish Rd ALDT GU11 ....2 C4
  FLEETS GU52 ....40 B3
Caves Farm Cl SHST GU47 ....11 G3
Cedar Av BLKW GU17 ....20 B1
Cedar Cl ASHV GU12 ....50 A2
  BAGS GU19 ....8 C5
Cedar Dr FLEETN GU51 ....36 A5
Cedar Gv CHOB/PIR GU24 ....25 G2
Cedar Rd FARN GU14 ....38 C1
Cedars Cl SHST GU47 ....11 F3
The Cedars FLEETS GU51 ....35 H4
Cedar Vw FLEETS GU52 ....40 D1
Cedarways FNM GU9 ....60 D1
Celandine Cl CWTH RG45 ....7 E2
Celandine Cl YTLY GU46 ....10 A4
Cemetery Pales
  CHOB/PIR GU24 ....33 G4
Cemetery Rd FLEETN GU51 ....35 E5
Centre Terrace Rd
  FARN GU14 ....38 A4
Centurion Cl SHST GU47 ....12 B3
Chaffinch Cl SHST GU47 ....12 C3
Chalfont Dr FARN GU14 ....38 C2
Chamber La RFNM GU10 ....52 C5
Chambers Rd ASHV GU12 ....44 D1
Chamomile Gdns FARN GU14 .....28 A4
Champion Wy FLEETS GU52 ......40 C2
Chandlers La YTLY GU46 ....10 D4
Chandlers Rd ASHV GU12 ....44 D3
Chantreys FLEETN GU51 ....34 D4
Chantry Cl FNM GU9 ....4 B4
Chantry Rd BAGS GU19 ....15 F1
The Chantrys FNM GU9 ....4 B5
Chapel Av BAGS GU19 ....15 F1
Chapel La BAGS GU19 ....15 F1
  CHOB/PIR GU24 ....33 G5
  FARN GU14 ....28 D1
Chapel Rd CBLY GU15 ....21 F1
  RFNM GU10 ....60 A5
Chapel Sq CBLY GU15 ....12 D5
Chapel St FARN GU14 ....29 H5
Chaplain's Hl CWTH RG45 ....7 F4
Charlecote Cl FARN GU14 ....38 D1
Charlesworth Pl FARN GU14 .....35 G1
Charlotte Cl FNM GU9 ....21 G1
Charlton Ct SHST GU47 ....12 B2
Chart House Rd ASHV GU12 ......39 G5
Chartwell FNM GU9 ....60 B2
  FRIM GU16 ....30 A4
Chartwell Gdns ALDT GU11 ......38 C5
The Chase CWTH RG45 ....6 C2
  FARN GU14 ....29 H3
Chatfield Cl FARN GU14 ....38 C2
Chatsworth Gv FNM GU9 ....47 H4
Chatsworth Hts CBLY GU15 ......14 C4
Chatsworth Rd FARN GU14 ......22 A5
Chatton Rw CHOB/PIR GU24......25 G4
Chaucer Cl CBLY GU15 ....21 H1
Chaucer Rd CWTH RG45 ....6 D4
  FARN GU14 ....28 D3
Chawton Cl FLEETN GU51 ....34 C1
Cheetah Rd FARN GU14 ....38 B2

Chelwood Dr SHST GU47 ....11 F2
Cherberry Cl FLEETN GU51 ......26 D5
Cheriton Wy BLKW GU17 ....20 B1
Cherrydale Rd CBLY GU15 ....23 F1
Cherryhill Gv ALDT GU11 ....2 A5
Cherry Ldg ASHV GU12 * 3 F4
Cherry Tree Cl FARN GU14 * 28 A4
  SHST GU47 ....12 B2
Cherry Tree Rd RFNM GU10 .....60 A5
Cherrywood Rd FARN GU10 ......29 E2
Chesilton Crs FLEETS GU52 .....40 C3
Chester Cl ASHV GU12 ....44 D5
Chester Rd ASHV GU12 ....44 D4
Chesters Rd CBLY GU15 ....22 D1
Chester Wy RFNM GU10 ....50 B4
Chestnut Av ASHV GU12 ....50 A3
  CBLY GU15 ....14 C5
  FNM GU9 ....53 G5
Chestnut Cl BLKW GU17 * 20 C1
  FLEETN GU51 ....27 E5
Chestnut Ct ALDT GU11 ....3 G3
Chestnut Gv FLEETN GU51 ....35 H2
Chestnut Rd FARN GU14 ....28 B4
Cheswell Gdns FLEETN GU51 .....40 A1
Chetwode Pl ALDT GU11 ....49 G3
Chetwode Ter ALDT GU11 ....48 C1
Cheviot Cl CBLY GU15 ....23 E2
  FARN GU14 ....28 A5
Cheviot Dr FLEETN GU51 ....26 D5
Cheviot Rd SHST GU47 ....11 F2
Chewter La BFOR GU20 ....9 F2
Cheylesmore Dr FRIM GU16 .....23 F5
Cheyne Wy FARN GU14 ....28 D2
Chichester Rd ASHV GU12 ....44 C4
Chilham Cl FRIM GU16 ....30 B1
Chillingham Wy CBLY GU15 ......21 G2
Chiltern Av FARN GU14 ....28 B5
Chiltern Cl FARN GU14 ....28 A5
  FLEETS GU52 ....40 D2
Chiltern Rd SHST GU47 ....11 F2
Chilton Farm Pk
  FARN GU14 ....28 A5
Chineham Cl FLEETN GU51 ......34 C1
The Chine RFNM GU10 ....60 B5
Chingford Av FARN GU14 ....29 G4
Chinnock Cl FLEETS GU52 ....35 F5
Chobham Rd FRIM GU16 ....22 A4
  WOKN/KNAP GU21 ....25 H1
Choiseley Dr FLEETN GU51 ......35 E1
Christmas Av ASHV GU12 * 1 H5
Christmas Pl ASHV GU12 ....3 H5
Christchurch Cl FLEETS GU52 ...40 B3
Christchurch Dr BLKW GU17 .....12 A5
Christie Cl LTWR GU18 ....16 B2
Christie Wk YTLY GU46 ....18 C2
Christine Cl ALDT GU11 ....50 B1
Christy Est ASHV GU12 * 44 A5
Church Av FARN GU14 ....38 C2
Church Cir FARN GU14 ....38 C2
Church Cl CHOB/PIR GU24 ......33 F2
Church Ct FLEETS GU51 ....35 F3
Church Gv FLEETN GU51 ....35 E3
Church Hll ALDT GU11 ....22 A1
Churchill Av ASHV GU12 ....3 G6
Churchill Crs FARN GU14 ....29 F2
Church La ASHV GU12 ....44 D5
  CHOB/PIR GU24 ....25 G2
  CHOB/PIR GU24 ....32 D4
  FARN GU14 ....29 H1
  RFNM GU10 ....58 A2
  RFNM GU10 ....60 A2
  RFNM GU10 ....60 B1
Church La East ALDT GU11 .....2 D5
Church La West ALDT GU11 .....2 B5
Church Pth ASHV GU12 ....44 C4
Church Rd ALDT GU11 ....3 G7
  BAGS GU19 ....8 B5
  BFOR GU20 ....9 F4
  CBLY GU15 ....12 D4
  CHOB/PIR GU24 ....17 F4
  FLEETN GU51 ....29 H1
  SHST GU47 ....12 A5
  YTLY GU46 ....12 B2
Church Rd East CWTH RG45 .....6 D3
  FARN GU14 ....38 D3
Church Rd West CWTH RG45 .....6 D4
  FARN GU14 ....38 C3
Church St ALDT GU11 ....2 B5
  CWTH RG45 ....6 D4
Church Vw ASHV GU12 ....10 D4
  YTLY GU46 ....10 D4
Circle Hill Rd CWTH RG45 .....7 E3
Clandon Ct FARN GU14 ....38 D1
Clanfield Ride BLKW GU17 ......20 B1
Clare Md RFNM GU10 ....60 B5
Claremont Av CBLY GU15 ....22 B1
Clarence Cl ASHV GU12 ....3 H3
Clarence Dr CBLY GU15 ....14 D4
Clarence Rd FLEETN GU51 ......35 F4
Clarendon Ct BLKW GU17 ....20 B3
Clarewood Dr CBLY GU15 ....14 A5
Clarke Crs CBLY GU15 ....12 C4
Clarks Hl RFNM GU10 ....52 C5
Claycart Rd ALDT GU11 ....42 B4
Claydon Gdns FARN GU14 ....28 A4
Clayton Barracks ALDT GU11 ....43 H3
Clayton Ct FNM GU9 * 5 F4
Clayton Rd FARN GU14 ....20 D4
Clearsprings LTWR GU18 ....15 H5
Cleeve Ct FARN GU14 ....38 D1
Cleveborough Dr CBLY GU15 .....14 C5
Clews La CHOB/PIR GU24 ....25 G3
Clifton Cl FNM GU9 ....60 D1
Clifton Gdns FRIM GU16 ....30 B3
Clitheroe Rd FARN GU14 ....29 F5
Clive Rd ASHV GU12 ....3 J5
Clockhouse Rd FARN GU14 ......29 F5
The Cloisters FRIM GU16 ....21 H5
The Close FNM GU9 ....5 K6
  FRIM GU16 ....29 H3
  LTWR GU18 ....16 A2

SHST GU47 ....12 C3
Closeworth Rd FARN GU14 ......39 E4
Clouston Rd FARN GU14 ....38 D4
Clover La YTLY GU46 ....10 A5
Clubhouse Rd ALDT GU11 ....42 D2
Club La CWTH RG45 ....7 F3
Clumps Rd RFNM GU10 ....61 G4
Coach House Cl
  FLEETN GU51 ....35 G1
Cobbets Rdg RFNM GU10 ....55 G5
Cobbetts Farm
  CHOB/PIR GU24 ....25 G2
Cobbett's La BLKW GU17 ....19 F2
Cobbetts Ms FNM GU9 * 4 E3
Cobbetts Wk CHOB/PIR GU24....25 G3
Cobbetts Wy FNM GU9 ....60 B2
Cochrane Pl BFOR GU20 ....9 H3
Cock-a-Dobby SHST GU47 ....11 G5
Cody Cl ASHV GU12 ....44 B2
Cody Rd FARN GU14 ....37 H1
Coe Cl ALDT GU11 ....2 C4
Cokenor Wd FNM GU9 ....48 A4
Colbeck FLEETS GU52 ....40 D3
Colfred Cnr FLEETN GU51 ....27 E5
Coldharbour La
  CHOB/PIR GU24 ....17 F3
Cold Harbour La FARN GU14 .....28 D1
Cole Av ALDT GU11 ....7 F3
Coleford Bridge Rd FRIM GU16 .29 H5
Coleford Ct FARN GU14 ....39 F1
Coleford Paddocks
  FRIM GU16 ....30 B5
Coleman Rd ASHV GU12 ....3 H6
Coleridge Av YTLY GU46 ....19 E1
Coleridge Cl CWTH RG45 ....6 D4
Coleson Hill Rd RFNM GU10 .....60 B3
Coleville Rd FARN GU14 ....28 D4
Colin Cl FNM GU9 ....60 D2
College Crs CBLY GU15 ....21 H3
College Crs SHST GU47 ....12 C3
College Gdns FNM GU9 ....4 E5
College Ride BAGS GU19 ....15 E1
  CBLY GU15 ....13 H4
College Rd ASHV GU12 ....44 C4
  SHST GU47 ....12 C4
Collier Cl FARN GU14 ....28 A4
Collingwood FARN GU14 ....39 E2
Collingwood Grange Cl
  CBLY GU15 ....14 C3
Collingwood Ri CBLY GU15 ......14 C4
Collins Gdns ASHV GU12 ....44 D5
Colne Av ASHV GU12 ....50 C1
Columbus Dr FARN GU14 ....37 E1
Colville Gdns LTWR GU18 ....16 D2
Colwyn Cl YTLY GU46 ....10 B5
Combe La FARN GU14 ....29 E5
Combe Ri FARN GU14 ....61 F3
Comet Cl ASHV GU12 ....44 B2
Comfrey Cl FARN GU14 ....28 A4
Commercial Rd ASHV GU12 ......3 H6
Commonfields
  CHOB/PIR GU24 ....17 F5
Compound Rd FARN GU14 ....38 A2
Compton Cl FLEETS GU52 ....40 D2
  FARN GU14 ....13 H2
Compton Rd FARN GU14 ....40 C2
Condor Rd FARN GU14 ....38 A4
Conifer Cl FLEETS GU52 ....40 B2
Conifer Ct FARN GU14 ....55 E3
The Conifers CWTH RG45 ....6 C1
Coniston Cl CBLY GU15 ....23 E3
  FARN GU14 ....13 H1
Coniston Ct ASHV GU12 * 44 B3
  LTWR GU18 ....16 B2
Coniston Dr FNM GU9 ....47 G4
Coniston Wy FLEETS GU52 ......40 A2
Connaught Barracks
  ALDT GU11 ....43 H1
Connaught Ct CWTH RG45 ......6 B5
  YTLY GU46 ....10 B5
Connaught Crs
  CHOB/PIR GU24 ....33 F2
  BAGS GU19 ....8 A5
  CBLY GU15 ....22 B1
  CHOB/PIR GU24 ....33 F2
  FLEETN GU51 ....35 G4
Connop Wy FRIM GU16 ....22 B3
Consort Dr CBLY GU15 ....15 E4
Constable Wy SHST GU47 ....12 C5
Constant Rd FARN GU14 ....36 C2
Conway Dr FARN GU14 ....38 A3
Cookham Cl SHST GU47 ....12 A2
Coolarne Ri CBLY GU15 ....14 D4
Coombe Cl FLEETN GU51 ....36 A3
Coombe Mnr
  CHOB/PIR GU24 ....25 H2
Coombe Rd YTLY GU46 ....10 B4
Cooper Rd BFOR GU20 ....9 H1
Coopers Hill Dr
  CHOB/PIR GU24 ....32 C2
Copelands Cl CBLY GU15 ....23 F2
Copped Hall Dr CBLY GU15 ......15 E5
Copped Hall Wy CBLY GU15 .....15 E5
Copperfield Av SHST GU47 ......12 C1
Coppice Cl FNM GU9 ....48 C4
Coppice Gdns CWTH RG45 ....6 B3
  YTLY GU46 ....18 C1
Copse Av FNM GU9 ....48 C3
Copse Cl CBLY GU15 ....22 C1
Copse End CBLY GU15 ....14 B5
The Copse FARN GU14 ....37 F1
  RFNM GU10 ....60 B2
Copse Wy RFNM GU10 ....60 B2
Copthorne Dr LTWR GU18 ....16 B2
Corbett Dr LTWR GU18 ....15 H4
Cordelia Gdns ASHV GU12 ......39 F4
Cordwalles Rd CBLY GU15 ....14 B3
Coresbrook Wy
  WOKN/KNAP GU21 ....25 H5
Corfe Gdns FRIM GU16 ....22 B5
Corfe Wy FARN GU14 ....39 E3
Coriander Cl FARN GU14 ....28 A5

Cormorant Pl SHST GU47 ....12 C3
Cornbunting Cl SHST GU47 ......12 B4
Cornelia Cl FARN GU14 ....38 C2
Cornfields YTLY GU46 ....18 B2
Cornwall Cl CBLY GU15 ....14 B4
Coronation Rd ALDT GU11 ....49 F3
  YTLY GU46 ....10 D4
Corringway FLEETS GU52 ....40 D1
Corsham Wy CWTH RG45 ....6 D2
Cotswold Cl FARN GU14 ....28 C2
Cotswold Rd SHST GU47 ....11 F2
Cottage Gdns FARN GU14 ....28 D5
Cottesloe Cl CHOB/PIR GU24....25 F3
Cotton Cl ALDT GU11 ....2 A1
Courtenay Rd FARN GU14 ....48 C4
Court Gdns CBLY GU15 ....21 H1
Courtmoor Av FLEETS GU52 .....35 F5
Court Rd ALDT GU11 ....2 D2
Cove Rd FARN GU14 ....28 B2
  FLEETN GU51 ....35 H1
Coverts Cl FNM GU9 ....54 C1
The Covert FARN GU14 ....28 C1
Covey Cl FARN GU14 ....28 C4
Covington Crs CHOB/PIR GU24 ..32 D2
Coxbridge Mdw FNM GU9 ....4 B5
Coxgreen SHST GU47 ....12 B2
Coxheath Rd FLEETS GU52 ......40 A1
Coxmoor Cl FLEETS GU52 ....41 E2
Crabtree Rd CBLY GU15 ....21 F4
Crake Pl SHST GU47 ....12 B3
Cranbrook Ct FLEETN GU51 .....35 G1
Crane Ct SHST GU47 ....12 B3
Cranford Av FLEETS GU52 ....40 A2
Cranford Park Dr YTLY GU46 ....10 D5
Cranleigh Ct FARN GU14 ....28 C4
Cranmore Cl ALDT GU11 ....48 C1
Cranmore La ALDT GU11 ....48 C1
Cranmore Gdns ALDT GU11 .....48 C2
Cranmore Rd FRIM GU16 ....30 B5
Cranwell Gv LTWR GU18 ....15 H5
Craven Cl RFNM GU10 ....61 E2
Crawford Gdns CBLY GU15 ......21 F1
Crawley Cl CBLY GU15 ....14 B5
Crawley Hl CBLY GU15 ....22 B1
Crawley Ridge CBLY GU15 ......14 B5
Crawley Wood Cl CBLY GU15 ....22 B1
Credon Cl FARN GU14 ....28 C4
Cree's Meadow BFOR GU20 * 9 H5
Crerar Cl FARN GU14 ....37 F1
Crescent La ASHV GU12 ....44 D2
The Crescent FARN GU14 ....38 C1
  FNM GU9 ....48 B2
  YTLY GU46 ....10 D4
Cricketers La BFOR GU20 ....9 H5
Cricket Field Gv CWTH RG45 ....7 F4
Cricket Hill La BLKW GU17 ......18 D5
  YTLY GU46 ....19 E1
Cricket La RFNM GU10 ....61 E3
Crimea Rd ALDT GU11 ....2 E3
Cripley Rd FARN GU14 ....28 C4
Crofters Cl SHST GU47 ....11 G3
Croft La YTLY GU46 ....10 C4
Croft Rd ALDT GU11 ....3 F7
Croft Wy FRIM GU16 ....22 B5
Cromwell Rd CBLY GU15 ....13 H4
Cromwell Wy FARN GU14 ....28 C4
Crondall Ct CBLY GU15 ....21 F2
Crondall End YTLY GU46 ....10 C4
Crondall La RFNM GU10 ....52 C3
Crondall Rd RFNM GU10 ....59 E1
Crookham Reach
  FLEETS GU52 ....40 A2
Crookham Rd FLEETN GU51 .....40 A1
Crooksbury Rd RFNM GU10 .....55 F2
Crosby Gdns YTLY GU46 ....10 A4
Crosby Hill Dr CBLY GU15 ......14 B4
Crosby Wy FNM GU9 ....54 C1
Cross Gdns FRIM GU16 ....30 B5
Cross La FRIM GU16 ....30 B5
Cross Rd ASHV GU12 ....44 D4
  FARN GU14 ....37 G3
Cross St ALDT GU11 ....2 D4
  FARN GU14 ....38 C4
Crossways ASHV GU12 ....3 H5
Crown Dr FNM GU9 ....49 E5
Crown Gdns FLEETN GU51 ......35 H4
Crown La FNM GU9 ....49 E5
Crown Pl SHST GU47 ....12 C2
Crowthorne Rd SHST GU47 ......11 H5
Croyde Cl FARN GU14 ....29 E3
Cruikshank Lea SHST GU47 ......12 C5
Cuckoo La CHOB/PIR GU24 ......16 D5
Cuckoo V CHOB/PIR GU24 ....16 D5
Cullen Cl YTLY GU46 ....18 C1
Cullens Ms ALDT GU11 * 2 C4
Culverlands Crs ASHV GU12 .....44 B4
Culver Rd SHST GU47 ....12 B2
Cumberland Rd CBLY GU15 ......23 E2
Cumbria Ct FARN GU14 ....39 E5
Cunnington Rd FARN GU14 ......38 A4
Curley Hill Rd LTWR GU18 ......15 C4
Curly Bridge Cl FARN GU14 .....28 D1
Curtis Cl CBLY GU15 ....15 E4
Curzon Br CHOB/PIR GU24 ......32 A4
Curzon Dr FLEETS GU52 ....40 C2
Cuthbert Rd ASHV GU12 ....44 C1
Cutts Rd ALDT GU11 ....38 D5
Cypress Gdns FARN GU14 ....20 D5
Cypress Rd FLEETN GU51 ....36 A3
Cyprians Av CHOB/PIR GU24 ....33 H5
Cyprus Rd FRIM GU16 ....31 F1

D

Daffodil Dr CHOB/PIR GU24 .....25 G3
Dairy Gate Rd FARN GU14 ....38 B4
Dale Cl RFNM GU10 ....60 B1
Dale Gdns SHST GU47 ....12 B4
Dalley Ct SHST GU47 ....12 B4
Dalston Cl CBLY GU15 ....23 F3
Damask Cl CHOB/PIR GU24 .....17 C5

Danvers Dr FLEETS GU52
Daphne Dr FLEETS GU52
Darby Green La BLKW GU17
Darleydale Ct SHST GU47
Dare's La RFNM GU10
Darset Av FLEETN GU51
Darracott Cl CBLY GU15
Darvills La FNM GU9
Darvills Rd FNM GU9
Darvills La FNM GU9
Darwin Gv ALDT GU11
Davis Gdns SHST GU47
Dawney Rd CBLY GU15
Dawney Hl CHOB/PIR GU24
Dawneys Rd CHOB/PIR GU24
Dawsmere Cl CBLY GU15
Deadbrook La ASHV GU12
Dean Pde CBLY GU15 *
Deans Ct BFOR GU20
Decouttere Cl FLEETN GU51
Deedman Cl ASHV GU12
Deepcut Bridge Rd
  FRIM GU16
Deepdene RFNM GU10
Deep Well Dr CBLY GU15
Deer Leap LTWR GU18
Deer Rock Rd CBLY GU15
Dell Gv FRIM GU16
The Dell FNM GU9
  YTLY GU46
Delville Cl FARN GU14
Dene Cl ASHV GU12
  RFNM GU10
Dene La RFNM GU10
Dene La West RFNM GU10
Dene Rd ALDT GU11
Dene Wk RFNM GU10
Denham Dr YTLY GU46
Denly Wy LTWR GU18
Denman Cl FLEETN GU51
Denmark Sq ASHV GU12
Denmark St ASHV GU12
Denning Ct FLEETS GU52
Dennistoun Cl CBLY GU15
Denton Wy FNM GU9
Derby Rd FARN GU14
Derwent Av ALDT GU11
Derwent Cl FARN GU14
  FNM GU9
Derwent Rd LTWR GU18
Dettingen Crs FRIM GU16
Dettingen Rd FRIM GU16
Devil's Highway The
  FNM GU9
Devon Cl FLEETN GU51
  SHST GU47
Devon Rd ALDT GU11
Devonshire Dr CBLY GU15
Devonshire Pl ALDT GU11
Dexter Wy FLEETN GU51
Diamond Hl CBLY GU15
Diamond Rdg CBLY GU15
Diamond Wy FARN GU14
Dickens Wy YTLY GU46
Dingley Wy FARN GU14
Dinorben Av FLEETS GU52
Dinorben Beeches
  FLEETS GU52
Dinorben Cl FLEETS GU52
Dippenhall Rd RFNM GU10
Dippenhall St RFNM GU10
Dogflud Wy FNM GU9
Dollis Dr FNM GU9
Doman Rd CBLY GU15
Donlan Dr FARN GU14
Donnafields CHOB/PIR GU24
Donnington Cl CBLY GU15
Dora's Green La RFNM GU10
  RFNM GU10
Dorcas Ct CBLY GU15
Doreen Cl FARN GU14
Dormer Cl CWTH RG45
Dorset Rd ASHV GU12
Douai Cl FARN GU14
Douglas Gv RFNM GU10
Dovedale Cl SHST GU47
Dowding Ct CWTH RG45 *
Downing St FNM GU9
Downs Cl FARN GU14
Doyle Gdns YTLY GU46 *
Drake Av FRIM GU16
Draynorse Dr BAGS GU19
Drifters Dr FRIM GU16
The Drive FNM GU9
Drovers End FLEETN GU51
Drovers Wy ASHV GU12
  FRIM GU16
Dryden Rd FARN GU14
Duchess Cl CWTH RG45
Duchess of Kent Barracks
  ALDT GU11
Duke of Cornwall Av
  CBLY GU15
Dukes Cl FNM GU9 *
Dukes Covert BAGS GU19
Dukes Hl BAGS GU19
Dukes Md FLEETS GU52
Dukes Pk ALDT GU11
Duke's Ride CWTH RG45
Dukes Wd CWTH RG45
Dumas Cl YTLY GU46
Du Maurier Cl FLEETS GU52
Dump Rd FARN GU14
Dunbar Rd FARN GU14
Dundaff Cl CBLY GU15
Dungells Farm Cl YTLY GU46
Dungells La YTLY GU46
Dunmow Hl FLEETN GU51
Dunsmore Gdns YTLY GU46
Dunstall Pk FARN GU14
Durham Dr FRIM GU16
Durham Rd SHST GU47
Durnsford Av FLEETS GU52
Duval Pl BAGS GU19

E

le Cl CWTH RG45 ....6 C1
les Nest SHST GU47 ....11 G2
l of Chester Dr FRIM GU16 ......31 F1
sbourne FLEETS GU52 ....40 D3
s Gv CBLY GU15 ....14 A5
t Av FNM GU9 ....48 B4
tern Av CHOB/PIR GU24 ....33 H5
tern La CWTH RG45 ....3 K3
tern Av CBLY GU12 ....3 K3
t Gn BLKW GU17 ....20 A2
tmead FARN GU14 ....29 F5
t Ring RFNM GU10 ....50 C5
t Station Rd ASHV GU12 ....2 E4
s St FARN GU14 ....5 G2
ay Rd ASHV GU12 ....21 F2
o Barn La RFNM GU10 ....60 A3
barrow Ct CWTH RG45 * 6 C1
barrowhill Star CWTH RG45 .....6 C5
barrow Wt SHST GU47 ....11 C1
cumbe Park Dr CWTH RG45 .....6 C3
edale Cl CWTH RG45 ....6 D4
meoor Rd RFNM GU10 ....23 E5
ewood Cl CWTH RG45 ....6 C1
ey Cl FLEETS GU52 ....40 D1
ward Av CBLY GU15 ....21 E1
ward Rd BFOR BG20 ....9 H4
FNM GU9 ....61 E1
ard St ALDT GU11 ....2 B5
moor Br ALDT GU11 ....42 A1
moor Plain Rd ALDT GU11 ....42 B3
moor Rd ALDT GU11 ....42 B2
FARN GU14 ....37 H2
rton Rd CBLY GU15 ....13 F5
ars Rd FRIM GU16 ....58 B5
ars Hl ALDT GU11 ....2 C7
leton Cl FLEETS GU52 ....40 A2
et Gdns ALDT GU11 ....49 E3
leton Cl CWTH RG45 ....6 C4
o Rd CHOB/PIR GU24 ....3 J5
ergrove FARN GU14 ....39 E2
er Rd CHOB/PIR GU24 ....61 F3
n Dr RFNM GU10 ....65 C2
ar Av CWTH RG45 ....6 D2
n Rd ASHV GU12 ....19 E5
n Wy FRIM GU16 ....30 B2
t Cl CBLY GU15 ....14 D4
abeth Av BAGS GU19 ....15 H1
beach Dr FLEETS GU52 ....40 C2
ns Gv RFNM GU10 ....60 D5
n Dr FLEETN GU51 ....26 D5
ray Ct ASHV GU12 ....14 A5
s Cl FARN GU14 ....38 B1
s Rd FARN GU14 ....38 A2
son Wy RFNM GU10 ....50 B5
Rd CWTH RG45 ....6 D2
s Bank YTLY GU46 ....10 C4
s Crs FNM GU9 ....48 B3
ecroft Cl FRIM GU16 ....30 B2
s Gv CHOB/PIR GU24 ....48 A3
FNM GU9 ....48 A5
a Grove Rd FARN GU14 ....29 F5
a La RFNM GU10 ....50 B2
a Pl ALDT GU11 ....3 G7
a Rd FNM GU9 ....48 B3
sleigh Rd FARN GU14 ....29 F5
s Rd ALDT GU11 ....2 D4
FLEETN GU51 ....36 A3
Elms BLKW GU17 * 11 G2
r Rd FRIM GU16 ....50 B3
RFNM GU10 ....50 C5
enwood Crs CBLY GU15 ....14 C5
enwood Dr CBLY GU15 ....14 C4
ey Cl FRIM GU16 ....30 D3
ead Rd RFNM GU10 ....50 C5
on PI ASHV GU12 ....3 G6
on Rd ASHV GU12 ....3 J6
etham Cl FLEETN GU51 ....35 F1
etham Cres FLEETN GU51 ....34 D1
etham Heath FLEETS GU51 .....34 D1
etham Heath Wy
etham Cl FLEETN GU51 ....34 D1
etham PI FLEETN GU51 ....35 E1
etham Rd FLEETN GU51 ....34 C1
ed FRIM GU16 ....30 C2
ery Down Dr FARN GU14 ....34 C1
press Av FARN GU14 ....29 F2
field Rd ASHV GU12 ....40 D2
plesfield Cl FARN GU14 ....23 E1
merdale Gv FNM GU9 ....47 G4
om Cl CBLY GU15 ....13 G3
s Rd FARN GU14 ....38 A4
ca Cl CHOB/PIR GU24 ....17 E5
rest Rd CBLY GU12 ....13 H5
CWTH RG45 ....6 D5
engreen Rd FRIM GU16 ....22 B4
ersley Dr FLEETN GU51 ....34 C1
esham Wk SHST GU47 ....12 A2
ins Cl ASHV GU12 ....44 C5
shot La FLEETS GU52 ....60 B4
ter Gdns YTLY GU46 ....10 B4
ter Rd ASHV GU12 ....44 C4
hibition Rd FARN GU14 ....38 A4

F

racres RFNM GU10 * 60 B4
rfax Ms FARN GU14 ....38 D2
rfax Rd FARN GU14 ....29 F2
Fairfield Dr FRIM GU16 ....22 A3
Fairfield La CHOB/PIR GU24 ....17 F4
The Fairfield FNM GU9 ....5 H4
Fairholme Gdns FNM GU9 ....5 H6
Fairland Cl FLEETS GU52 ....35 H4
Fairmead Ct SHST GU47 ....12 C4
Fairmead Cl CBLY GU15 ....21 G2
Fairmile FLEETS GU52 ....40 C1
Fairview Gdns FNM GU9 ....44 B3
Fairview Rd ASHV GU12 ....44 D4
Fairway Hts CBLY GU15 ....14 D5
The Fairway FARN GU14 ....58 C4
FNM GU9 ....48 B5
FRIM GU16 ....31 G2
Fakenham Wy SHST GU47 ....12 B2
Falaise Cl ALDT GU11 ....2 B5
Falcon Cl LTWR GU18 ....15 H3
Falcon Wy YTLY GU46 * 10 B5
Falkner Rd FNM GU9 ....4 D3
Falkners Cl FLEETS GU52 ....27 E5
Fallowfield FLEETN GU51 ....27 E5
YTLY GU46 ....10 B4
Falmouth Cl CBLY GU15 ....22 C2
Faraday Rd FARN GU14 ....29 G5
Farcrosse Cl SHST GU47 ....12 A3
Fareham Dr YTLY GU46 ....10 B4
Faringdon Cl SHST GU47 ....12 A2
Farley Ct FARN GU14 * 38 D2
Farm Cl CWTH RG45 ....18 D1
YTLY GU46 ....18 D1
Farm Ct FRIM GU16 * 21 F5
Farm Dr FLEETN GU51 ....26 D5
Farm Rd ASHV GU12 ....44 A4
FARN GU14 ....22 A4
FRIM GU16 ....18 D1
Farm Vw YTLY GU46 ....18 D1
Farm Wk ASHV GU12 ....18 D1
Farnborough Ga FARN GU14 * ...29 G2
Farnborough Rd ALDT GU11 ....2 A1
ALDT GU11 ....43 E2
FARN GU14 ....38 D2
Farnborough St FARN GU14 .....29 H4
Farnham By-Pass FNM GU9 ....4 B7
Farnham Park Cl FNM GU9 ....47 H4
Farnham Rd FLEETN GU51 ....36 B5
Farrell Cl CBLY GU15 ....21 G3
Faulkner PI BAGS GU19 ....28 A2
Faversham Rd SHST GU47 ....12 B2
Felbridge Cl FRIM GU16 ....30 B3
Fellow Gn CHOB/PIR GU24 ......17 F5
Fellow Green Rd
CHOB/PIR GU24 ....17 F5
Fellows Rd FARN GU14 ....38 D3
Fennel Cl FARN GU14 ....29 F1
Fennscombe Ct
CHOB/PIR GU24 ....17 E5
Fenns La CHOB/PIR GU24 ....17 E5
Ferbies FLEETS GU52 ....40 C1
Fermor Dr ALDT GU11 ....2 E1
Fernbrae Cl RFNM GU10 ....62 D1
Fern Cl CWTH RG45 ....6 D1
FRIM GU16 ....23 E3
Ferndale Rd FLEETS GU52 ....40 B2
Ferndown Gdns FARN GU14 .....28 C5
Fern Dr FLEETN GU51 ....40 A5
Fernhill Cl FARN GU14 ....20 C5
FNM GU9 ....47 H4
Fernhill Dr FNM GU9 ....47 H4
Fernhill La FARN GU14 ....47 H4
FNM GU9 ....47 H5
Fernhill Rd FARN GU14 ....20 C4
FARN GU14 ....28 C2
Fernhill Wk FARN GU14 ....20 D5
Ferniehurst CBLY GU15 ....14 D5
Fernleigh Ri FRIM GU16 ....31 E2
Ferns Mead FNM GU9 ....4 D6
The Ferns FNM GU9 * 48 A5
Field End CHOB/PIR GU24 ....17 F5
FARN GU14 ....54 D1
Fieldfare Av YTLY GU46 ....10 A5
Fielding Gdns CWTH RG45 ....6 B4
Fielding Rd SHST GU47 ....12 C5
Field La FRIM GU16 ....22 A5
Field Rd FARN GU14 ....20 D5
Field Stores Ap ALDT GU11 ....3 G1
Field Wy ASHV GU12 ....44 A5
RFNM GU10 ....50 B3
Fieldway FLEETN GU51 ....34 D4
Fifield La RFNM GU10 ....63 E1
Fincham End Dr CWTH RG45 .....6 B4
Findhorn Cl SHST GU47 ....12 B4
The Findings FARN GU14 ....28 C1
Finney Dr BFOR GU20 ....9 H4
Fintry PI FARN GU14 ....28 C2
Fir Acre Rd ASHV GU12 ....44 C1
Fir Cl FLEETS GU52 ....51 E1
Fir Dr BLKW GU17 ....20 B3
Fire Station Rd ALDT GU11 ....2 E1
Fire Thorn Cl FLEETS GU52 ....40 B1
Firfield Rd FNM GU9 ....60 C1
Firglen Dr YTLY GU46 ....10 D4
Firgrove Ct FNM GU9 ....5 G5
Firgrove Hl FNM GU9 ....5 K6
Firgrove Pde FARN GU14 * 29 F5
Firgrove Rd FARN GU14 ....29 F5
HTWY RG27 ....10 A5
Firlands Av CBLY GU15 ....21 H1
Firs Cl FARN GU14 ....38 C2
Firtree Cl SHST GU47 ....11 F5
Firtree Wy FLEETN GU51 ....35 H4
Firwood Dr CBLY GU15 ....14 D5
Fishermen's Cl ALDT GU11 ....44 A2
Fitzroy Rd FLEETN GU51 ....27 E5
The Flats BLKW GU17 ....19 H2
Fleet Rd ALDT GU11 ....41 H1
FARN GU14 ....27 H5
FLEETN GU51 ....33 F5
FLEETS GU52 ....35 F3
FLEETS GU52 ....36 B5
Fleming Cl FARN GU14 ....29 H5
Florence Cl YTLY GU46 ....10 C5
Florence Rd FLEETS GU52 ....40 D1
SHST GU47 ....12 C4
Foden Rd ALDT GU11 ....2 D4
Folly Cl FLEETS GU52 ....51 E1
Folly Hl FNM GU9 ....47 G5

Folly La North FNM GU9 ....47 H3
Folly La South FNM GU9 ....47 G4
The Polly LTWR GU18 * 16 B4
Fontwell Cl ALDT GU11 ....3 J2
Forbes Cha SHST GU47 ....12 B4
Ford La RFNM GU10 ....60 D2
Ford Rd CHOB/PIR GU24 ....25 F2
Foreman Rd ASHV GU12 ....44 D5
Foreman Rd ASHV GU12 ....44 D5
Forest Dean FLEETN GU51 ....27 E5
Forest Dr RFNM GU10 ....61 E4
Forest End Rd SHST GU47 ....11 F2
Forest End Rd SHST GU47 ....11 F2
Foresters Wy CWTH RG45 ....18 A4
Forest Gld RFNM GU10 ....59 H5
Forest Hills CBLY GU15 ....21 F2
Forest Rd CWTH RG45 ....7 E5
Forge Cl FNM GU9 ....5 K1
Forge La FARN GU14 ....42 D1
Forth Cl FARN GU14 ....28 B3
Fortrose Cl SHST GU47 ....12 B4
Fosseway CWTH RG45 ....6 B3
Fossewood Dr CBLY GU15 ....13 H5
Fosters Gv BFOR GU20 ....9 F2
Fowler Av FARN GU14 ....38 B2
Fowler Rd FARN GU14 ....37 H2
Fowler's Rd ALDT GU11 ....43 G2
Fox Covert LTWR GU18 ....16 A3
Fox Cft FLEETS GU52 ....40 D2
Foxdown Cl CBLY GU15 ....21 G1
Fox Dr YTLY GU46 ....10 D4
Fox Heath FARN GU14 ....37 E1
Foxhill Crs CBLY GU15 ....14 D5
Fox Hills La ASHV GU12 ....45 E4
Foxhurst Rd ASHV GU12 ....44 C3
Foxley Cl BLKW GU17 ....20 A1
Fox Rd RFNM GU10 ....60 D5
Fox Wy RFNM GU10 ....46 D2
Foxwood FLEETS GU52 ....36 A1
Fox Yd FNM GU9 ....4 E3
Foye La FLEETS GU52 ....40 D2
France Hill Dr CBLY GU15 ....21 G1
Fraser Md SHST GU47 ....12 C5
Frederick St ALDT GU11 ....2 E3
Freelands Dr FLEETS GU52 ....40 A2
Freemantle Rd BAGS GU19 ....28 B5
Freesia Dr CHOB/PIR GU24 ......25 G3
French Gdns RFNM GU10 ....20 B2
Frenchmans Creek
FLEETS GU52 ....40 A3
Frensham Av FLEETN GU51 ......36 A3
Frensham Cl YTLY GU46 ....10 B5
Frensham Ct RFNM GU10 ....60 D4
Frensham Heights Rd
RFNM GU10 ....62 C1
Frensham Rd CWTH RG45 ....18 A4
RFNM GU10 ....61 F4
Frensham V RFNM GU10 ....61 E4
Frere Av FARN GU14 ....35 E5
Frestwood Dr YTLY GU46 ....18 C2
Friars Fld FNM GU9 ....4 E2
Friend Av ASHV GU12 ....3 K5
Friesian Cl FARN GU14 ....37 H1
Frimley Green Rd FRIM GU16 ....30 A2
Frimley Grove Gdns
FRIM GU16 ....21 H5
Frimley Hall Dr CBLY GU15 ......14 B5
Frimley High St FRIM GU16 ......21 H5
Frimley Rd CBLY GU15 ....21 F2
FRIM GU16 ....21 F2
Frith Hill Rd FRIM GU16 ....22 C5
Frodsham Wy SHST GU47 ....12 C1
Frogmore Gv BFOR GU20 ....20 A2
Frogmore Park Dr BLKW GU17 ..20 A2
Frogmore Rd BLKW GU17 ....19 H1
Frome Cl FARN GU14 ....28 B3
Fromow Gdns BFOR GU20 ....9 H4
Fry's La YTLY GU46 ....11 E4
Fuchsia Wy CHOB/PIR GU24 ....17 E5
Fugelmere Rd FLEETN GU51 .....36 A2
Fullers Rd RFNM GU10 ....59 H4
Furse Cl CBLY GU15 ....22 D2
Further Vell-Mead
FLEETS GU52 ....40 A3
Furze Cl ASHV GU12 ....39 G5
Furze Hill Crs CWTH RG45 ....7 E4
Fyfield Cl BLKW GU17 ....20 B1

G

Gable End FARN GU14 * 29 F5
Gables Cl ASHV GU12 ....44 C2
FARN GU14 ....29 E5
Gables Rd FLEETS GU52 ....40 B3
Gabriel Dr CBLY GU15 ....22 D2
Gaffney Cl ALDT GU11 ....38 D5
Gainsborough Cl CBLY GU15 ....14 B4
FARN GU14 ....38 D2
Gale Barracks ALDT GU11 * 45 F3
Gale Dr LTWR GU18 ....16 A2
The Galleries ALDT GU11 * 2 D2
The Gallop YTLY GU46 ....10 D4
Galloway Cl FLEETN GU51 ....27 E5
Gallwey Rd ALDT GU11 ....43 G4
Gally Hill Rd FLEETS GU52 ....40 B3
Galwey Rd YTLY GU46 ....18 C2
Gapemouth Rd
CHOB/PIR GU24 ....32 A4
FNM GU9 ....31 G4
Garbetts Wy RFNM GU10 ....50 A4
Garden Cl FARN GU14 ....37 G2
Gardener's Hill Rd RFNM GU10 ..60 A2
Gardenia Ct CHOB/PIR GU24 ....17 F5
The Gardens CHOB/PIR GU24 ...33 F4
RFNM GU10 ....50 B3
Garfield Rd CBLY GU15 ....21 G1
Garnet Fld YTLY GU46 ....10 B3
Garrick Wy FRIM GU16 ....30 A3
Garth Cl FNM GU9 ....60 C1
The Garth ASHV GU12 ....50 B1
FNM GU9 ....60 C1
The Gates FLEETN GU51 ....27 E5

George Gdns ALDT GU11 ....49 C3
Georgeham Rd FLEETN GU47 ....12 B1
George Rd FLEETN GU51 ....35 H3
George St CHOB/PIR GU24 ....32 A3
Georgian Cl CBLY GU15 ....14 A4
Germander Dr CHOB/PIR GU24 ..25 G3
Gibbet La CBLY GU15 ....21 G1
Gibbons Cl SHST GU47 ....12 A4
Gibb's Acre CHOB/PIR GU24 ....33 F5
Gibbs Wy YTLY GU46 ....18 B2
Giffard Dr FARN GU14 ....28 D3
Giffards Meadow FNM GU9 ......54 C4
Gilbert Rd FRIM GU16 ....31 F1
Gillian Av ASHV GU12 ....3 H6
Gillian Cl ASHV GU12 ....3 J6
Girton Cl SHST GU47 ....12 C2
The Glade FNM GU9 ....48 B4
FRIM GU16 ....39 F2
Gladiator Wy FARN GU14 ....38 A4
Glamis Cl FRIM GU16 ....30 B2
Glebe Cl ALDT GU11 ....49 E3
LTWR GU18 ....16 A1
Glebe Ct FLEETN GU51 ....35 F5
Glebeland Rd CBLY GU15 ....20 D2
Glebe Rd FARN GU14 ....28 D4
The Glebe BLKW GU17 ....20 C2
Glenavon Gdns YTLY GU46 ......18 D2
Glencoe Cl FRIM GU16 ....30 B1
Glendale Pk FLEETN GU51 ....34 C2
Gleneagles Dr FARN GU14 ....37 E1
Glenhurst BFOR GU20 ....9 E2
Glenhurst Cl BLKW GU17 ....20 C2
Glen Innes SHST GU47 ....12 C2
Glenmount Rd FRIM GU16 ....39 G2
Glen Rd FLEETN GU51 ....35 F4
The Glen FNM GU9 ....48 A4
Globe Farm La BLKW GU17 ......19 H1
Glorney Md FNM GU9 ....54 C4
Gloucester Cl FRIM GU16 ....30 A5
Gloucester Rd ALDT GU11 ....49 G3
BAGS GU19 ....8 C5
Glynswood CBLY GU15 ....22 B3
FNM GU9 ....49 E4
Goddards La CBLY GU15 ....21 F5
Godfrey Cl SHST GU47 ....12 B4
Goldcrest Cl YTLY GU46 ....10 B5
Goldfinch Cl ALDT GU11 ....2 B7
Goldhill RFNM GU10 ....61 G1
Gold La ALDT GU11 ....44 A3
Goldney Rd CBLY GU15 ....22 D2
Goldsmith Wy CWTH RG45 ....6 A4
Gole Rd CHOB/PIR GU24 ....32 D3
Golf Dr CBLY GU15 ....22 D2
Gondreville Gdns FLEETS GU52 ..40 A3
Gong Hl RFNM GU10 ....61 F5
Gong Hill Dr RFNM GU10 ....61 F4
Goodden Crs FARN GU14 ....37 H2
Goodwood Cl CBLY GU15 ....13 G3
Goodwood Pl FARN GU14 ....39 E1
Gordon Av CBLY GU15 ....21 F1
FLEETS GU52 ....40 D1
Gordon Crs CBLY GU15 ....21 G1
Gordon Rd ALDT GU11 ....2 D4
CBLY GU15 ....21 F1
CWTH RG45 ....7 F5
FARN GU14 ....38 D4
Gordon Wk YTLY GU46 ....19 E1
Gorse Bank LTWR GU18 * 16 A3
Gorse Cl FNM GU9 ....60 C2
Corselands YTLY GU46 ....18 C2
Gorselands Cl ASHV GU12 ....44 C2
Gorse La RFNM GU10 ....60 C2
Gorse Rd FRIM GU16 ....22 A4
Gorseway RFNM GU10 ....59 H4
Gort Cl ALDT GU11 ....43 F5
Gosden Rd CHOB/PIR GU24 .....17 F5
Cosnell Cl FRIM GU16 ....23 F3
Gough Rd FLEETN GU51 ....35 E2
Gough's Meadow SHST GU47 ...11 H4
Government House Rd
ALDT GU11 ....38 A5
Government Rd ALDT GU11 ......44 A5
Governor's Rd CBLY GU15 ....12 D5
Govett Gv BFOR GU20 ....9 H3
Gower Pl SHST GU47 ....12 B4
Grace Bennett Cl FARN GU14 * ..29 E2
Graham Rd BFOR GU20 ....9 F2
Grampian Rd SHST GU47 ....11 F1
Grand Av CBLY GU15 ....13 G5
Grange Av CWTH RG45 ....6 D2
Grange Ct RFNM GU10 * 50 A2
Grange Farm Rd ASHV GU12 ....44 C4
Grange Rd ASHV GU12 ....50 D1
CBLY GU15 ....22 A1
CHOB/PIR GU24 ....32 D4
FLEETN GU51 ....40 B2
FLEETS GU52 ....40 B2
FNM GU9 ....50 A4
Grantham Cl SHST GU47 ....12 C4
Grantley Cl FNM GU9 ....60 B2
Grantley Dr FLEETS GU52 ....35 F5
Grant Rd CWTH RG45 ....7 E5
Grasmere Rd FARN GU14 ....37 G1
FNM GU9 ....47 G4
LTWR GU18 ....16 B2
Gravel Hill Rd RFNM GU10 ....58 D4
Gravel Rd FARN GU14 ....38 D4
FLEETS GU52 ....40 D1
FNM GU9 ....47 H3
Grayshott Dr BLKW GU17 ....20 A1
Grayswood Dr FRIM GU16 ....39 G3
Great Austins FNM GU9 ....5 J7
Great Elms Rd RFNM GU10 ....5 J7
Greatfield Cl FARN GU14 ....29 E1
Greatfield Rd FARN GU14 ....29 E1
Green Acre ALDT GU11 ....2 A7
Greenacres RFNM GU10 ....55 G5
Greencroft FARN GU14 ....29 F5
Green End YTLY GU46 ....10 D4
Green Farm Rd BAGS GU19 ......28 B5
Greenfield Rd FARN GU14 ....29 E1
Greenfield Wy CWTH RG45 ....6 C1
Green Glades FLEETS GU52 ....40 B2
Greenhaven YTLY GU46 ....18 B1
Green Hill Cl CBLY GU15 ....15 E5

Greenhill Cl FNM GU9 ....60 C1
Greenhill Rd FNM GU9 ....54 B5
Greenhill Wy FNM GU9 ....60 C2
Greenholme CBLY GU15 ....23 F1
Greenlands Rd CBLY GU15 ....21 F5
Green La BAGS GU19 ....11 H2
BLKW GU17 ....19 H2
BLKW GU17 ....20 A1
BLKW GU17 ....20 C2
FNM GU9 ....48 D4
FNM GU9 ....50 D2
FRIM GU9 ....62 A5
RFNM GU10 ....12 A3
YTLY GU46 ....10 B4
Green Lane Cl CBLY GU15 ....13 C4
Green La West ASHV GU12 ....51 C2
Greenleas FRIM GU16 ....22 A4
Greenleas Cl YTLY GU46 ....10 C4
Green Leys FLEETS GU52 ....40 B3
Greensand Wy FNM GU9 ....5 H4
Greenside CWTH RG45 ....6 E3
The Green FNM GU9 ....49 F4
FNM GU9 ....30 B3
RFNM GU10 ....56 A4
Green Wy ASHV GU12 ....44 A4
Greenways FLEETS GU52 ....40 B1
FRIM GU16 ....11 H2
Greenwood Rd
CHOB/PIR GU24 ....32 B3
CWTH RG45 ....6 C2
Grenadier Rd ASHV GU12 ....44 D3
Grenadiers Wy FARN GU14 ......37 E1
Grenville Dr FLEETN GU51 ....35 E5
Grenville Gdns FRIM GU16 ....30 A3
Gresham Wy FRIM GU16 ....30 A3
Greville Cl ALDT GU11 ....2 C2
Greyfriars Dr CHOB/PIR GU24 ..25 G2
Greyhound Cl ASHV GU12 ....50 B1
Greys Ct ALDT GU11 ....42 C5
Greystead Pk RFNM GU10 ....60 A2
Greystoke Ct CWTH RG45 ....6 C4
Grieve Cl RFNM GU10 ....50 A5
Griffon Cl FARN GU14 ....37 F1
Grindstone Crs
WOKN/KNAP GU21 ....25 H5
Grosvenor Ct BLKW GU17 ....20 B3
Grosvenor Rd ALDT GU11 ....2 C5
Grove Cl EWKG RG40 ....6 A1
Grove Cross Rd FRIM GU16 ....21 H5
Grove End BAGS GU19 ....8 D4
Grove End Rd FNM GU9 ....5 J1
Grove Farm Pk FRIM GU16 * 59 F3
Grovefields Av FRIM GU16 ....21 H5
Grovelands RFNM GU10 ....61 G1
Grove Rd ASHV GU12 ....44 C5
CBLY GU15 ....22 A1
FLEETS GU52 ....40 D1
The Grove ALDT GU11 ....2 D4
FARN GU14 ....38 D3
FRIM GU16 ....21 H5
Guernsey Dr FLEETN GU51 ....26 D5
Guildford Rd ALDT GU11 ....49 H5
ASHV GU12 ....5 F4
BAGS GU19 ....8 C5
CHOB/PIR GU24 ....17 E4
CHOB/PIR GU24 ....33 F5
FLEETS GU51 ....36 A3
FNM GU9 ....4 E6
FNM GU9 ....30 C4
LTWR GU18 ....16 B2
RFNM GU10 ....55 E1
Guildford Rd East FARN GU14 ...38 C3
Guildford Rd West FARN GU14 ..38 C3
Guillemont Fids FARN GU14 ......28 B4
Gulley Rd FARN GU14 ....38 A4
Gun Hl ALDT GU11 ....2 E1

H

Habershon Dr FRIM GU16 ....23 F4
Hadleys RFNM GU10 ....60 A5
Hadrians FNM GU9 ....54 C1
Hagley Rd FLEETN GU51 ....35 E2
Haig La FLEETS GU52 ....40 D2
Haig Rd ASHV GU12 ....3 H4
CBLY GU15 ....13 H5
Hailsham Cl SHST GU47 ....12 B2
Haining Gdns FRIM GU16 ....39 C1
Halebourne La CHOB/PIR GU24 ..17 G2
Hale Pl FNM GU9 ....48 C5
Hale Reeds FNM GU9 ....48 B4
Hale Rd FNM GU9 ....5 K1
Hale Wy FRIM GU16 ....21 H5
Halifax Cl FARN GU14 ....37 H1
Halifax Wy FARN GU14 ....37 H5
Halimote Rd ALDT GU11 ....2 D4
Hall Cl CBLY GU15 ....14 A5
Hall Dr FLEETS GU52 ....40 D1
Hall Farm Crs YTLY GU46 ....18 C1
Hallgrove Bottom BAGS GU19 ...8 D3
Hall La YTLY GU46 ....18 C1
Hallmark Cl SHST GU47 ....12 C3
Hall Rd FARN GU14 ....38 B3
Hamble Av BLKW GU17 ....20 B1
Hambleton Cl CBLY GU15 ....22 D3
Hamesmoor Rd FRIM GU16 ......30 A5
Hamesmoor Wy FRIM GU16 ......30 B5
Hamilton Pl ALDT GU11 ....2 A7
Hamilton Rd FLEETS GU52 ....40 D1
Hamlash La RFNM GU10 ....63 E2
Hammersley Rd ALDT GU11 ......38 B5
Hammond Wy LTWR GU18 ....16 B2
Hampshire Cl ASHV GU12 ....44 B3
Hampshire Rd CBLY GU15 ....14 B5
Hampton Cl FLEETS GU52 ....40 C3
Hampton Rd FNM GU14 ....47 C4
Hanbury Wy CBLY GU15 ....21 C3
Hancombe Rd SHST GU47 ....11 C1
Handford La YTLY GU46 ....18 C2
Hangerfield Cl YTLY GU46 ....18 C2

Hanover Cl FRIM GU16 ...... 22 A5
  YTLY GU46 ...... 10 D4
Hanover Dr FLEETN GU51 ...... 27 E5
Hanover Gdns FARN GU14 ...... 28 C3
Hanson Cl CBLY GU15 ...... 14 D4
Harbour Cl FARN GU14 ...... 29 E1
Harcourt Rd CBLY GU15 ...... 21 F1
Hardy Av YTLY GU46 ...... 18 C2
Hardy Gn CWTH RG45 ...... 6 C4
Harlech Rd BLKW GU17 ...... 20 B2
Harlington Wy FLEETN GU51 ...... 35 E4
Harpdon Pde YTLY GU46 ...... 10 D4
Harper's Rd ASHV GU12 ...... 45 E5
Harpton Cl YTLY GU46 ...... 10 D4
Hart Cl FARN GU14 ...... 28 C1
Hart Dene Ct BAGS GU19 ...... 8 C5
Hartford Ri CBLY GU15 ...... 13 H5
Hartland Pl FARN GU14 ...... 29 E2
Hartley Cl BLKW GU17 ...... 19 H1
Hartsleaf Cl FLEETN GU51 ...... 35 F4
Harts Leap Cl SHST GU47 ...... 11 G2
Harts Leap Rd SHST GU47 ...... 11 G3
The Hart FNM GU9 ...... 4 E5
Harvard Rd SHST GU47 ...... 12 D2
Harvest Cl YTLY GU46 ...... 18 B2
Harvest Crs FLEETN GU51 ...... 26 D4
Harvey Rd FARN GU14 ...... 28 A4
Haslemere Ct FRIM GU16 ...... 23 E3
Hastings Cl FRIM GU16 ...... 30 C2
The Hatches FNM GU9 ...... 53 F5
  FRIM GU16 ...... 30 B3
Hatch Ride CWTH RG45 ...... 6 D1
Hatfield Ct CBLY GU15 ...... 21 F1
Hatfield Gdns FARN GU14 ...... 39 E1
Hatherwood YTLY GU46 * 19 F1
Hatton Hl BFOR GU20 ...... 9 G3
Haven Wy FNM GU9 ...... 54 B1
Haweswater Ct ASHV GU12 * 44 B3
Hawker Rd ASHV GU12 ...... 44 B2
Hawkes Leap BFOR GU20 ...... 9 F2
Hawkesworth Dr BAGS GU19 ...... 15 F2
Hawkins Wy FLEETS GU52 ...... 36 A4
Hawkswood Av FRIM GU16 ...... 22 B4
Hawkwell FLEETS GU52 ...... 40 D5
Hawley Gn BLKW GU17 ...... 20 C3
Hawley Gv BLKW GU17 ...... 20 C4
Hawley La FARN GU14 ...... 29 F1
Hawley Rd BLKW GU17 ...... 20 C3
Hawthorn Cl ASHV GU12 ...... 50 A2
Hawthorn Ct FARN GU14 ...... 38 C4
Hawthorne Crs BLKW GU17 ...... 20 C2
Hawthorn La RFNM GU10 ...... 60 B5
Hawthorn Rd FNM GU9 ...... 54 B1
Hawthorn Wy CHOB/PIR GU24 ...... 25 G3
Haywood Dr FLEETS GU52 ...... 35 G5
Hazel Av FARN GU14 ...... 37 H2
Hazel Rd FNM GU9 ...... 4 A4
Hazel Rd ASHV GU12 ...... 51 E3
  FRIM GU16 ...... 59 G2

Hearmon Cl YTLY GU46 ...... 18 B3
Hearsey Gdns BLKW GU17 ...... 11 H5
Heath Cl FARN GU14 ...... 48 A3
Heathcote Cl ASHV GU12 * 44 C4
Heathcote Rd ASHV GU12 ...... 44 D4
  CBLY GU15 ...... 21 H1
Heath Dr CHOB/PIR GU24 ...... 31 H1
Heather Cl ALDT GU11 ...... 44 C4
  ASHV GU12 ...... 44 D2
  FNM GU9 ...... 60 B2
Heatherdale Rd CBLY GU15 ...... 21 G2
Heatherdene Av CWTH RG45 ...... 6 A4
Heather Dr FLEETS GU52 ...... 40 B2
Heatherley Cl CBLY GU15 ...... 21 F1
Heather Rd FNM GU9 ...... 53 E1
Heather Rd FRIM GU16 ...... 22 B4
Heathermount Dr CWTH RG45 ...... 6 B2
Heather Wk CHOB/PIR GU24 ...... 32 D3
Heatherway CWTH RG45 ...... 6 C5
Heathfield Ct FLEETN GU51 ...... 35 E5
Heath Hill Rd North CWTH RG45 ...... 6 D3
Heath Hill Rd South CWTH RG45 ...... 6 D3
Heathland St ALDT GU11 ...... 2 D3
Heath La FNM GU9 ...... 48 A3
  RFNM GU10 ...... 46 A4
Heath Ri BAGS GU19 * 8 C5
Heath Ri CBLY GU15 ...... 21 H1
Heathside Pk CBLY GU15 ...... 15 E4
Heathvale Bridge Rd
  ASHV GU12 ...... 44 C1
Heathway CBLY GU15 ...... 21 H1
Heathway Cl CBLY GU15 ...... 21 H1
Heathwood Cl YTLY GU46 ...... 10 D4
Heathyfields Rd FNM GU9 ...... 47 F4
Heddon Wk FARN GU14 ...... 38 C4
Hedgecroft YTLY GU46 * 10 B5
Heenan Cl FRIM GU16 ...... 30 A2
Helen Ct FARN GU14 ...... 29 F5
Helksham Cl SHST GU47 ...... 12 B2
Henley Cl FARN GU14 ...... 30 A2
Henley Dr FRIM GU16 ...... 30 A2
Henley Gdns YTLY GU46 ...... 18 D1
Hepworth Cft SHST GU47 ...... 12 C5
Herbert Rd FLEETN GU51 ...... 35 E3
Herbs End FARN GU14 ...... 28 A4
Hereford La FNM GU9 ...... 47 H4
Hereford Rd FLEETN GU51 ...... 26 D5
Hermes Cl FLEETN GU51 ...... 36 A5
Hermitage Cl FARN GU14 ...... 38 D3
  FRIM GU16 ...... 22 B5
Heron Cl FLEETS GU52 ...... 41 E1
  FRIM GU16 ...... 30 B5
Heronscourt LTWR GU18 ...... 16 E3
Heronscroft LTWR GU18 ...... 16 C3
Herons Wy CHOB/PIR GU24 ...... 32 D3
Heron Wood Rd ASHV GU12 ...... 3 K7
Herretts Gdns ASHV GU12 ...... 3 H5
Herrett St ASHV GU12 ...... 3 J6
Herrick Ct FRIM GU16 ...... 23 E3
Herrings La BFOR GU20 ...... 9 H3
Hewlett Pl BAGS GU19 ...... 8 C5
Hexham Cl SHST GU47 ...... 12 C1
Heywood Dr BAGS GU19 ...... 15 E1

Hicks La BLKW GU17 ...... 19 H1
Higgs La BAGS GU19 ...... 8 B5
High Beeches FRIM GU16 ...... 21 H4
Highbury Crs CBLY GU15 ...... 14 C4
Highclere Dr CBLY GU15 ...... 14 C4
Highclere Rd ASHV GU12 ...... 3 J6
Highdown FLEETN GU51 ...... 35 G2
Highfield Av ALDT GU11 * 2 D7
Highfield Ct ALDT GU11 ...... 2 E7
  FARN GU14 ...... 28 D5
  FNM GU9 ...... 60 D1
Highfield Gdns ALDT GU11 ...... 2 D7
Highfield Pth FARN GU14 ...... 28 D5
Highfield Rd FARN GU14 ...... 28 D5
Highgate La FARN GU14 ...... 29 G4
Highgrove FARN GU14 ...... 29 F2
Highland Dr FLEETN GU51 ...... 35 H1
Highland Rd ASHV GU12 ...... 3 J5
  CBLY GU15 ...... 14 A3
Highlands Cl FARN GU14 ...... 29 E5
Highlands Cl FNM GU9 ...... 60 D1
Highlands Rd FARN GU14 ...... 48 A3
High Park Rd FNM GU9 ...... 5 F2
High St ALDT GU11 ...... 2 C2
  ASHV GU12 ...... 3 J4
  BAGS GU19 ...... 8 C5
  CBLY GU15 ...... 13 H5
  CHOB/PIR GU24 ...... 17 E4
  CWTH RG45 ...... 6 D4
  FARN GU14 ...... 38 C4
  RFNM GU10 ...... 60 A5
  SHST GU47 ...... 11 F3
High View Cl FARN GU14 ...... 29 E5
Highview Crs CBLY GU15 ...... 14 A2
High View Rd FARN GU14 ...... 29 E5
  LTWR GU18 ...... 15 C5
Highway FARN GU14 ...... 29 E5
Highwayman's Rdg BFOR GU20 ...... 9 F2
Highwood Cl YTLY GU46 ...... 18 C2
Highworth FLEETS GU52 ...... 6 D2
Hilder Gdns FARN GU14 ...... 29 E5
Hilfield BLKW GU17 ...... 19 H1
Hillary Cl FNM GU9 ...... 60 D1
Hillary Rd FARN GU14 ...... 28 B3
Hillbrook Ri FNM GU9 ...... 47 G4
Hill Cl FARN GU14 ...... 20 D5
Hillcrest FARN GU14 * 28 D5
  FNM GU9 * 48 B2
Hill Crest Dr RFNM GU10 ...... 60 A5
Hillcrest Rd CBLY GU15 ...... 14 D4
Hill Rd FNM GU9 ...... 48 A1
Hillsborough Ct FARN GU14 ...... 28 C3
Hillsborough Pk CBLY GU15 ...... 23 E1
Hill School RFNM GU10 ...... 60 B4
Hillside CBLY GU15 ...... 13 F5
Hillside Crs FRIM GU16 ...... 30 B2
Hillside La FNM GU9 ...... 48 B3
Hillside Rd ALDT GU11 ...... 2 B7
  ASHV GU12 ...... 44 D4
  FNM GU9 ...... 48 C3
  RFNM GU10 ...... 60 D5
Hilltop Vw YTLY GU46 ...... 18 B1
Hill View Rd FNM GU9 ...... 4 B5
Hinaidi Wy FARN GU14 ...... 37 H4
Hindell Cl FARN GU14 ...... 29 E1
Hinstock Ct FARN GU14 ...... 38 A1
Hinton Cl CWTH RG45 ...... 6 D1
Hinton Dr CWTH RG45 ...... 6 D1
Hitches La FLEETN GU51 ...... 34 C5
H Jones Crs ALDT GU11 ...... 2 C4
Hogarth Cl SHST GU47 ...... 12 C5
Hoghatch La FNM GU9 ...... 47 G4
Holbeche Cl YTLY GU46 ...... 18 A1
Holbreck Cl ASHV GU12 * 44 C4
Holbrook Wy ALDT GU11 ...... 49 F3
Holder Rd ASHV GU12 ...... 50 A1
Hole La RFNM GU10 ...... 58 A3
Holland Cl FNM GU9 ...... 4 C1
Holland Gdns FLEETN GU51 ...... 35 G4
The Hollies FARN GU14 * 20 D5
Hollis Wood Dr RFNM GU10 ...... 60 A3
Holly Av FRIM GU16 ...... 22 D3
Hollybank CHOB/PIR GU24 ...... 17 F5
Hollybush La ALDT GU11 ...... 39 E5
Hollybush Tr BFOR GU20 ...... 8 D2
Holly Cl CWTH RG45 * 6 B3
  FARN GU14 ...... 3 H3
Holly Ct CWTH RG45 * 7 E5
Hollyfields Cl CBLY GU15 ...... 21 F1
Holly Hedge Cl FRIM GU16 ...... 22 A4
Holly Hedge Rd FRIM GU16 ...... 22 A4
Holly Hock CHOB/PIR GU24 ...... 32 D3
Holly Rd ASHV GU12 ...... 3 H5
  FARN GU14 ...... 28 D5
Hollytree Gdns FRIM GU16 ...... 29 H1
Hollytrees FLEETN GU51 ...... 40 A1
Holly Wy BLKW GU17 ...... 20 B2
Holmbrook Cl FARN GU14 ...... 28 A5
Holmbury Av CWTH RG45 ...... 6 C1
Holme Cl CWTH RG45 ...... 6 C1
Holt Cl FARN GU14 ...... 29 G2
Holt Pound La RFNM GU10 ...... 59 G3
Holton Cl CWTH RG45 ...... 6 D1
Holwell Cl FARN GU14 ...... 28 C5
Home Farm Cl FARN GU14 ...... 29 H3
Homelea Cl FARN GU14 ...... 29 F1
Homeleigh Crs ASHV GU12 ...... 39 G4
Home Park Rd YTLY GU46 ...... 10 C5
Homeside Cl FNM GU9 ...... 47 G4
Honeysuckle Cl CWTH RG45 ...... 6 C1
  YTLY GU46 ...... 18 A5
Honister Gdns FLEETN GU51 ...... 36 A2
Hook La CHOB/PIR GU24 ...... 16 C5
Hook Mill La CHOB/PIR GU24 ...... 16 D1
Hookstile La FNM GU9 ...... 5 G1
Hookstone La CHOB/PIR GU24 ...... 16 A1
Hope Fountain CBLY GU15 ...... 22 B2
Hope Grant's Rd ALDT GU11 ...... 2 E1
Hope La FNM GU9 ...... 47 H4
Hopeman Cl SHST GU47 ...... 12 B4
Hope Wy ALDT GU11 ...... 2 C1
Hop Gdn FLEETS GU52 ...... 40 A3
Hormer Cl SHST GU47 ...... 12 B4
Hornbeam Cl FARN GU14 ...... 28 A4
  SHST GU47 ...... 12 B4
Horn Rd FARN GU14 ...... 28 C4

Horsebrass Dr BAGS GU19 ...... 15 G1
Horseshoe Cl CBLY GU15 ...... 14 B5
Horseshoe Crs CBLY GU15 ...... 14 B5
Horseshoe La CBLY GU15 ...... 14 B5
Horsham Rd SHST GU47 ...... 12 B2
Hospital Hl ALDT GU11 ...... 2 C1
Hospital Rd ALDT GU11 ...... 43 E4
Hostel Rd FARN GU14 ...... 38 B4
Houlton Ct BAGS GU19 ...... 15 G1
Houseman Rd FARN GU14 ...... 28 D5
Howard Cl FLEETN GU51 ...... 36 A3
Howard Cole Wy ALDT GU11 ...... 42 C4
Howard Rd ASHV GU12 ...... 27 H5
Howes Gdns FLEETN GU51 ...... 40 A1
The Howe FARN GU14 ...... 36 D3
Huddington Gld HTWY RG27 ...... 34 A1
Humber Wy SHST GU47 ...... 12 B5
Hungerford Cl SHST GU47 ...... 12 A3
Hunnels Ct FLEETS GU52 ...... 40 A4
Hunter Rd FARN GU14 ...... 37 H1
Huntsman's Ms FRIM GU16 ...... 30 B5
Hurlands Cl FARN GU14 ...... 54 D1
Hurlands Pl FARN GU14 ...... 54 D1
Hurricane Wy FARN GU14 ...... 37 H5
Hurst Rd ALDT GU11 ...... 43 G4
  FARN GU14 ...... 29 F1
Hussar Ct ALDT GU11 ...... 42 C5
Hutton Cl BFOR GU20 ...... 9 H5
Hutton Rd ASHV GU12 ...... 44 C1

I

Iberian Wy CBLY GU15 ...... 14 C5
Ilex Cl YTLY GU46 ...... 10 B5
Imjin Cl ALDT GU11 ...... 3 F1
Imran Ct ASHV GU12 ...... 3 G6
Ingle Dell CBLY GU15 ...... 21 H2
Inglewood Av CBLY GU15 ...... 23 F1
Innisfail Gdns ALDT GU11 ...... 2 B7
Institute Rd ASHV GU12 ...... 3 J6
Inverness La FARN GU14 ...... 29 E2
Inverness Wy SHST GU47 ...... 12 B4
Invincible Rd FARN GU14 ...... 38 A1
Iris Rd CHOB/PIR GU24 ...... 25 G2
Irvine Dr FARN GU14 ...... 28 C1
Isis Wy SHST GU47 ...... 12 B3
Ively Rd FARN GU14 ...... 37 E5
Ives Cl YTLY GU46 ...... 10 B4
Ivydene WOKN/KNAP GU21 ...... 25 H5
Ivy Dr LTWR GU18 ...... 16 A4
Ivy La FNM GU9 ...... 5 F3
Ivy Rd ASHV GU12 ...... 44 A3

J

Jacob Rd CBLY GU15 ...... 13 E4
Jaguar Rd FARN GU14 ...... 38 B2
James Rd ALDT GU11 ...... 38 D5
  CBLY GU15 ...... 21 F4
James Wy CBLY GU15 ...... 21 F4
Jays Nest Cl BLKW GU17 ...... 20 B3
Jenkins' Hill London Rd
  BAGS GU19 ...... 15 E2
Jenner Dr CHOB/PIR GU24 ...... 17 G5
Jenny's Wk YTLY GU46 ...... 19 F1
Jerome Cnr CWTH RG45 ...... 7 E5
Jersey Brow Rd FARN GU14 ...... 38 A2
Jersey Cl FLEETS GU52 ...... 26 D5
Jersey Cl BLKW GU17 ...... 19 F1
Jessett Dr FLEETS GU52 ...... 40 D5
John Cl ALDT GU11 ...... 48 C2
Johnson Wy FLEETS GU52 ...... 40 B1
Jubilee Dr FARN GU14 ...... 28 A5
Jubilee Dr ASHV GU12 ...... 44 C1
Jubilee Hall Rd FARN GU14 ...... 28 A5
Jubilee La RFNM GU10 ...... 60 C5
Jubilee Rd ALDT GU11 ...... 49 F5
  FRIM GU16 ...... 39 G2
Junction Rd LTWR GU18 ...... 16 B2
Juniper Dr CHOB/PIR GU24 ...... 25 G2
Juniper Rd FARN GU14 ...... 28 A4

K

Keable Rd RFNM GU10 ...... 60 B1
Keats Wy CWTH RG45 ...... 6 D1
  YTLY GU46 ...... 18 B2
Keble Wy SHST GU47 ...... 12 C1
Keith Lucas Rd FARN GU14 ...... 37 H2
Kelsey Cl YTLY GU46 ...... 19 F1
Kemp Ct BAGS GU19 ...... 15 H1
Kempton Ct FARN GU14 ...... 37 H2
Kendal Cl FARN GU14 * 28 C5
Kendal Gv CBLY GU15 ...... 23 F2
Kenilworth Crs FLEETN GU51 ...... 36 A2
Kenilworth Rd FARN GU14 ...... 28 C5
  FLEETN GU51 ...... 35 H3
Kenmore Cl FLEETS GU52 ...... 40 D2
Kennedy Cl FLEETS GU52 ...... 40 D5
Kennel La BFOR GU20 ...... 9 G3
Kennels La FARN GU14 ...... 36 D1
Kennet Cl ASHV GU12 ...... 50 C1
  FARN GU14 ...... 28 A4
Kentigern Dr CWTH RG45 ...... 7 G5
Kenton Cl FRIM GU16 ...... 22 B4
Kent Rd BFOR GU20 ...... 9 H5
  FLEETN GU51 ...... 35 H5
Kenwith Av FLEETN GU51 ...... 36 A3
Kenworth Dr CWTH RG45 * 6 D5
Keogh Barracks RFNM GU16 ...... 39 G4
Keogh Cl FRIM GU16 ...... 39 H5
Kepple Pl BAGS GU19 ...... 8 C5
Kerria Wy CHOB/PIR GU24 ...... 17 F5
Kerry Cl FLEETN GU51 ...... 26 D4
Kestrel Cl RFNM GU10 ...... 46 D5

Kestrel Rd FARN GU14 ...... 38 B2
Keswick Cl CBLY GU15 ...... 23 E2
Keswick Dr LTWR GU18 ...... 16 B5
Kevins Dr YTLY GU46 ...... 11 E4
Kevins Gv FLEETN GU51 ...... 35 H3
Keynes Cl FLEETS GU52 ...... 40 D5
Keynsham Wy SHST GU47 ...... 12 B1
The Key FLEETN GU51 ...... 54 D1
Kilmartin Gdns FRIM GU16 ...... 22 B5
Kilmore Dr CBLY GU15 ...... 22 D2
Kilmuir Cl SHST GU47 ...... 12 B4
Kiln La ALDT GU11 ...... 61 E2
Kiln Rd FNM GU9 ...... 48 B5
The Kilns FNM GU9 * 48 B5
Kiln Wy ALDT GU11 ...... 61 E2
Kimberley FLEETS GU52 ...... 40 D3
Kimbers La FNM GU9 ...... 5 K1
Kimpton Dr FLEETN GU51 ...... 34 C1
Kingcup Dr CHOB/PIR GU24 ...... 25 G2
Kingfisher Cl FARN GU14 ...... 28 A3
  FLEETS GU52 ...... 40 C2
Kingfisher Dr YTLY GU46 ...... 10 B5
Kingfisher Wk ASHV GU12 ...... 44 B4
King George Cl FARN GU14 ...... 38 D2
Kings Apartments CBLY GU15 ...... 22 D1
King's Av CHOB/PIR GU24 ...... 32 D1
  RFNM GU10 ...... 50 A2
Kingsclear Pk CBLY GU15 ...... 21 H2
King's Ct RFNM GU10 ...... 50 A2
King's Crs CBLY GU15 ...... 15 D5
Kingscroft FLEETN GU51 ...... 35 G4
Kings Keep FLEETS GU52 ...... 40 C1
  SHST GU47 ...... 11 H2
Kingsla FLEETN GU51 ...... 60 B2
Kingsley Av CBLY GU15 ...... 21 G2
Kingsley Cl CWTH RG45 ...... 6 C5
Kingsley Rd FARN GU14 ...... 28 D3
Kingsmead FARN GU14 ...... 29 F5
  FRIM GU16 ...... 30 A2
Kings Pde FLEETN GU51 * 35 G2
King's Ride CBLY GU15 ...... 13 H2
King's Rd ALDT GU11 ...... 48 C1
  CHOB/PIR GU24 ...... 25 G1
  CWTH RG45 ...... 6 D4
  FARN GU14 ...... 38 C1
Kingston Rd CBLY GU15 ...... 14 C5
King's Wk CBLY GU15 ...... 12 D5
Kingsway ALDT GU11 ...... 2 A5
  BLKW GU17 ...... 20 C2
Kipling Ct YTLY GU46 ...... 18 C2
Kirkham Cl SHST GU47 ...... 12 B1
Kirkstone Cl CBLY GU15 ...... 23 F2
Kirriemuir Gdns ASHV GU12 ...... 45 F4
Kitchener Rd ALDT GU11 ...... 43 H1
Knightsbridge Rd CBLY GU15 ...... 14 A4
Knights Rd FARN GU14 ...... 48 C5
Knights Wy CBLY GU15 ...... 23 E2
Knoll Cl FLEETN GU51 ...... 35 G2
Knoll Ct FLEETN GU51 ...... 35 G1
Knoll Rd CBLY GU15 ...... 13 H5
  FLEETN GU51 ...... 35 G1
Knollys Rd ALDT GU11 ...... 42 D4
The Knook SHST GU47 * 12 B4
Knowles Av CWTH RG45 ...... 6 B4
Knox Cl FLEETS GU52 ...... 40 A2
Kohat Ct ALDT GU11 ...... 2 C4
Kohima Cl ALDT GU11 ...... 3 F1
Krooner Rd CBLY GU15 ...... 21 F3

L

Laburnum Cl ALDT GU11 ...... 2 C4
Laburnum Pas ALDT GU11 ...... 2 C3
Laburnum Rd ALDT GU11 ...... 2 C4
  FNM GU9 ...... 48 C5
The Laburnums BLKW GU17 ...... 19 H1
Ladywood Av FARN GU14 ...... 28 A5
Laffan's Rd ALDT GU11 ...... 42 D2
Laffan Tr ALDT GU11 ...... 42 A1
Laird Ct BAGS GU19 ...... 15 G2
Lake End Wy CWTH RG45 ...... 6 D1
Lakeland Dr FRIM GU16 ...... 22 A5
Lake La RFNM GU10 ...... 62 A5
Lake Rd FRIM GU16 ...... 30 C3
Lakeside Cl ASHV GU12 ...... 44 C1
Lakeside Ct FLEETN GU51 ...... 35 H1
Lakeside Gdns FARN GU14 ...... 28 B2
Lakeside Rd ALDT GU11 ...... 38 A5
  ASHV GU12 ...... 44 C1
The Lake Side BLKW GU17 ...... 20 B2
Lambert Crs BLKW GU17 ...... 20 A2
Lamborne Cl SHST GU47 ...... 11 G2
Lambourne Dr BAGS GU19 ...... 15 F1
Lambourne Wy RFNM GU10 ...... 50 A3
Lanark Cl FRIM GU16 ...... 22 A4
Lancaster Av FNM GU9 ...... 5 H7
Lancaster Cl ASHV GU12 ...... 44 A3
Lancaster Dr CBLY GU15 ...... 13 H5
Lancaster Rd FARN GU14 ...... 38 B5
Lancaster Wy FARN GU14 * 29 G2
Lancer Ct ALDT GU11 * 42 C5
Landseer Cl SHST GU47 ...... 12 C5
Langdale Av FARN GU14 * 44 B2
Langdon Cl CBLY GU15 ...... 23 E2
Langley Ct FLEETS GU52 ...... 40 D3
Langley Dr ALDT GU11 ...... 49 E4
  CBLY GU15 ...... 13 H5
Lansdowne Rd ALDT GU11 ...... 2 C4
  FRIM GU16 ...... 30 C1
Larch Cl CBLY GU15 ...... 14 A2
Larchfield Rd FLEETS GU52 ...... 40 B2
Larch Wy FARN GU14 ...... 37 E1
Larchwood Gld CBLY GU15 ...... 14 C4
Larkfield Cl FNM GU9 ...... 4 A3
Larkfield Rd FNM GU9 ...... 4 A3
Larkswood Cl SHST GU47 ...... 11 G2
Larkswood Dr CWTH RG45 ...... 6 D5
Larmer Cl FLEETN GU51 ...... 34 D5
Latchwood La RFNM GU10 ...... 61 F3
Latham Av FRIM GU16 ...... 22 A4
Lauder Cl FRIM GU16 ...... 22 A4

Lauderdale FARN GU14 ...... 37 H5
Laundry La CBLY GU15 ...... 20 D5
Laurel Cl CBLY GU15 ...... 21 H2
Laurel Ct CBLY GU15 ...... 37 H5
  FNM GU9 1
Laurel Gdns ALDT GU11 ...... 49 H5
Laurel Gv RFNM GU10 ...... 60 C3
The Laurels FLEETN GU51 ...... 35 E3
  FNM GU9 1
Lavender La RFNM GU10 ...... 60 B2
Lawday Link FNM GU9 ...... 47 G4
Lawday Pl FNM GU9 ...... 47 G4
Lawday Place La FNM GU9 ...... 47 G4
The Lawns FNM GU9 ...... 10 B4
The Lawns CBLY GU15 1
Lawrence Crs BFOR GU20 9
Lawrence Rd FLEETS GU52 ...... 35 G5
Laws Ter ALDT GU11 ...... 3 H1
Lea Cl ASHV GU12 ...... 52 D1
  FNM GU9 1
Lea Ct FNM GU9 ...... 48 B2
Lea Cft CWTH RG45 ...... 7 E5
Lea Springs FLEETN GU51 ...... 34 D5
The Lea FLEETN GU51 ...... 35 E5
Lea Wy ASHV GU12 ...... 44 A3
Leaway FNM GU9 * 49 H5
Leawood Rd FLEETN GU51 ...... 34 D5
Lee Wood Rd FLEETN GU51 ...... 34 D5
Le Borowe FLEETS GU52 40
Lee Ct ALDT GU11 42
Lee Rd ALDT GU11 ...... 42 D4
Leger Cl FLEETS GU52 ...... 40 D5
Legge Crs ALDT GU11 ...... 48 C4
Leigh La FNM GU9 ...... 54 C1
Leipzig Barracks FLEETS GU52 ...... 40 D5
Leipzig Rd FLEETS GU52 ...... 40 D5
Leith Cl CWTH RG45 ...... 6 D1
Leith Dr ALDT GU11 2
Le Marchant Rd FRIM GU16 ...... 22 B5
Lendore Rd FRIM GU16 ...... 29 H1
Lennel Gdns FLEETS GU52 ...... 41 E1
Leonard Cl FRIM GU16 ...... 29 H3
Leopold Av FARN GU14 28
Lestock Wy FLEETN GU51 ...... 35 G2
Levern Dr FNM GU9 ...... 48 A2
Lewisham Wy SHST GU47 ...... 12 B4
Leycester Cl BFOR GU20 ...... 9 G3
Ley Rd FARN GU14 ...... 29 E1
Leyside CWTH RG45 6
Library Rd FARN GU14 ...... 38 C3
Lickfolds Rd RFNM GU10 ...... 62 A5
Lightwater Meadow
  LTWR GU18 ...... 16 A4
Lightwater Rd LTWR GU18 ...... 16 A4
Lille Barracks ALDT GU11 ...... 38 D5
Lime Av CBLY GU15 1
Limecroft YTLY GU46 ...... 18 B1
Limecroft Rd
  WOKN/KNAP GU21 25
Lime Dr FLEETN GU51 ...... 26 D4
Limes Rd FARN GU14 ...... 28 C5
Lime St ALDT GU11 2
Lincoln Cl ASHV GU12 ...... 44 A3
  CBLY GU15 ...... 23 F2
Lincoln Rd FARN GU14 ...... 38 B5
Linden Ct CBLY GU15 ...... 14 D4
The Lindens FNM GU9 5
Lindum Dene ALDT GU11 2
Ling Dr LTWR GU18 ...... 15 H5
Lingmala Gv FLEETS GU52 41
Link Rd FARN GU14 ...... 37 H5
Links Wy FARN GU14 ...... 37 E5
The Link YTLY GU46 ...... 10 D4
Linkway CBLY GU15 ...... 21 H1
  CWTH RG45 6
  FLEETS GU52 ...... 40 D3
Linsford La FRIM GU16 ...... 39 H1
Linstead Rd FARN GU14 ...... 28 A5
Lion & Lamb Wy FNM GU9 ...... 4 C4
Lion & Lamb Yd FNM GU9 * 4 C4
Lion Rd FARN GU14 ...... 28 C4
Lion Wy FLEETS GU52 ...... 40 C5
Liskeard Dr FARN GU14 ...... 28 C5
Lismoyne Cl FLEETN GU51 ...... 35 E3
Little Austins Rd FNM GU9 ...... 5 H5
Little Copse FLEETS GU52 41
  FNM GU9 10
Littlefield Cl ASHV GU12 ...... 44 C4
Littlefield Gdns ASHV GU12 ...... 50 D1
Little Green La FNM GU9 ...... 60 D1
Little Moor SHST GU47 12
Little Paddock CBLY GU15 ...... 14 C4
Little Thurbans Cl FNM GU9 ...... 60 D2
Little Vigo YTLY GU46 ...... 18 B3
Little Wellington St ALDT GU11 2
Littleworth Rd RFNM GU10 ...... 56 D1
Littleworth Rd FNM GU9 60
Llangar Gv CWTH RG45 6
Lobelia Rd CHOB/PIR GU24 ...... 25 G2
Lock Rd ALDT GU11 ...... 43 H1
Lockswood CHOB/PIR GU24 ...... 33 H5
Lockwood Cl FARN GU14 ...... 28 A4
Loddon Cl CBLY GU15 23
Loddon Rd FARN GU14 ...... 28 A4
Loddon Wy ASHV GU12 ...... 50 C1
Lodge Cl FARN GU14 11
Lodge Gv YTLY GU46 10
Lodge Hill Cl RFNM GU10 ...... 61 E3
Lodge Hill Rd RFNM GU10 ...... 61 E3
Lodsworth FARN GU14 ...... 37 H5
Loman Rd FRIM GU16 ...... 30 D3
Londlandes FLEETS GU52 ...... 40 D3
London Rd BFOR GU20 ...... 9 H5
  BLKW GU17 ...... 20 A2
  CBLY GU15 ...... 13 H5
Longacre ASHV GU12 ...... 44 A3
Long Av CHOB/PIR GU24 ...... 33 H5
Long Beech Dr FARN GU14 ...... 37 E1
Long Br FNM GU9 5
Longcroft RFNM GU10 58
Longdown FLEETS GU52 ...... 40 D3
Longdown Cl RFNM GU10 ...... 60 D5
Longdown Rd RFNM GU10 ...... 60 D5
  SHST GU47 11
Longfield Cl FARN GU14 ...... 28 A4
Longfield Rd ASHV GU12 50

gford Cl CBLY GU15 ....21 H2
g Garden Pl FNM GU9 ....5 F2
g Garden Wk FARN GU14 ....5 F3
g Garden Wk East FNM GU9 ....5 F3
g Garden Wk West
FNM GU9 ....5 F2
g HI RFNM GU10 ....56 A4
ghope Dr FRIM GU10 ....60 C2
gleat Sq FARN GU14 ....59 E1
gley Rd FNM GU9 ....5 J5
gmead FLEETS GU52 ....40 C1
gmeadow FRIM GU16 ....22 B3
g Mickle SHST GU47 ....11 G2
Long Rd RFNM GU10 ....60 B5
aine Rd CBLY GU15 ....14 B3
r Rdg BAGS GU19 ....8 C4
ian Rd CHOB/PIR GU24 ....32 A3
se Margaret Rd ALDT GU11 ....1 F1
ells Cl LTWR GU18 ....16 B2
rs La RFNM GU10 ....63 E4
e Cl ALDT GU11 ....2 A1
er Broadmoor Rd
WTH RG45
er Canes YTLY GU46 ....10 A5
er Church La FNM GU9 ....5 F4
er Church Rd SHST GU47 ....11 E2
er Farnham Rd ALDT GU11 ....49 J5
er Mill Fld BAGS GU19 ....15 F1
er Moor YTLY GU46 ....18 D1
er Mount St FLEETS GU51 ....34 C1
er Nelson St ALDT GU11 ....2 C2
er Newport Rd ASHV GU12 ....3 K6
er Sandhurst Rd
NM GU9 ....10 A1
er South Vw FNM GU9 ....5 F4
er Terrace Rd FARN GU14 ....38 A4
er Weybourne La
FNM GU9 ....48 D4
field Cl CTWR GU18 ....16 A5
lands Rd BLKW GU17 ....20 A2
La FNM GU9 ....49 F4
rnds Buildings FNM GU9 ....5 F2
ry Cl SHST GU47 ....12 B5
wood Av FLEETN GU51 ....35 E5
as Cl YTLY GU46 ....18 D1
as Green Rd
CHOB/PIR GU24 ....28 D2
ow Cl FRIM GU16 ....30 C2
altine Cl FARN GU14 ....48 C2
e Rd East FNM GU9 ....29 E2
worth Cl FARN GU14 ....29 E2
on Cl BAGS GU19 ....15 F1
l Pl FNM GU9 ....47 H3
n Gate Cl SHST GU47 ....11 F1
ford Cl FARN GU14 * 29 F1
FRIM GU16 ....30 C2
Copse Av FARN GU14 ....29 F1
ington Av YTLY GU46 ....18 C1
ams FLEETS GU52 ....40 A4
chford Rd ALDT GU11 ....38 D4
ch Rd FNM GU9 ....5 K4
dale Dr FLEETS GU51 ....36 B3
dford Ter FLEETS GU51 ....2 A1
dhurst Av BLKW GU17 ....12 A5
NM GU9 ....49 G4
dsey Cl FARN GU14 ....27 H5
eham Rd CWTH RG45 ....6 D3
n Wy FARN GU14 ....28 D2
ton Cl FNM GU9 ....60 C1
n Rd CWTH RG45 ....6 D3
n Wy FRIM GU16 ....9 G4
ander Wy FARN GU14 ....38 B3
ons Av ASHV GU12 ....39 F4
ons Rd ALDT GU11 ....2 D4

M

adam Av CWTH RG45 * 7 F1
donald Rd FNM GU9 ....45 H3
TWR GU18 ....15 H3
naghten Woods
CBLY GU15 ....14 A5
rae Rd YTLY GU46 ....18 D1
ney Rd FLEETS GU52 ....40 D1
dox Brown End SHST GU47 ....12 C5
azine Rd FARN GU14 ....37 H4
dalene Rd SHST GU47 ....12 B1
da Rd FLEETS GU51 ....12 B2
nolia Wy YTLY GU46 * 10 B5
pie Cl RFNM GU10 ....46 D2
uire Dr FRIM GU16 ....23 E3
onia Cl CHOB/PIR GU24 * 17 F5
da Rd ALDT GU11 ....48 B3
n Gate Rd FARN GU14 ....38 B2
nstone Cl FRIM GU16 ....31 E2
nstone Crs CHOB/PIR GU24 ....32 D3
nstone Rd CHOB/PIR GU24 ....25 F3
tland Rd FARN GU14 ....38 B2
tlands Cl RFNM GU10 ....50 A4
ard Cl ASHV GU12 ....44 B5
Mallards FRIM GU16 ....21 E5
thouse La CHOB/PIR GU24 ....17 F4
vern Rd BLKW GU17 ....11 J4
FARN GU14 ....28 B2
ndora Rd ALDT GU11 ....43 F3
field Rd ASHV GU12 ....44 C5
iley Bridge Rd RFNM GU10 ....50 A4
hor Cl RFNM GU10 ....50 B5
hor Crs CHOB/PIR GU24 ....60 C3
hor Farm ASHV GU12 * 50 B1
hor Gdns FRIM GU16 ....61 F3
hor Park Dr YTLY GU46 ....11 E5

Manor Park Est ASHV GU12 * 3 G4
Manor Rd ALDT GU11 ....2 B6
FARN GU14 ....58 D1
FNM GU9 ....54 C1
RFNM GU10 ....50 B2
Manorside Cl RFNM GU10 ....50 B2
Manor Wk ASHV GU12 ....2 E5
Manor Wy BAGS GU19 ....15 C1
Maple Cl ASHV GU12 ....59 F5
BLKW GU17 ....20 A1
SHST GU47 ....11 F2
Maple Dr CWTH RG45 ....7 E1
LTWR GU18 ....15 H3
Maple Gdns YTLY GU46 ....18 D1
Maple Leaf Cl FARN GU14 ....37 H1
Maple Wk ASHV GU12 ....3 K7
Mardale CBLY GU15 ....23 E2
Mareth Cl ALDT GU11 ....20 D1
Marigold Cl CWTH RG45 ....6 B1
Marigold Dr CHOB/PIR GU24 ....25 C2
Marjoram Cl FARN GU14 ....24 D1
Markham Ct CBLY GU15 ....13 H5
Marlborough Cl FLEETN GU51 ....36 B4
Marlborough Ri CBLY GU15 ....14 A5
Marrowbrook Cl FARN GU14 ....38 A1
Marrowbrook La FARN GU14 ....57 H2
Marshall Cl FARN GU14 ....28 D4
FRIM GU16 ....23 F4
Marshall Rd SHST GU47 ....12 B4
Marshwood Rd LTWR GU18 ....16 D3
Marston Dr FARN GU14 ....29 F2
Marston Rd FNM GU9 ....4 B5
Martel Cl CBLY GU15 ....15 E4
Martindale Av CBLY GU15 ....13 J6
Martingale Cl ALDT GU11 ....42 C5
Martins Cl BLKW GU17 ....20 B2
Martin Wy FRIM GU16 ....22 A5
Maskell Wy FARN GU14 ....57 E1
Mason Cl YTLY GU46 ....19 E1
Mason Pl SHST GU47 ....11 F3
Mason Rd FARN GU14 ....28 C4
Mason Wy ALDT GU11 ....49 F5
Matthews Ter ALDT GU11 * 3 G2
Matthew Rd FNM GU9 ....5 H7
Matthews Rd CBLY GU15 ....14 B3
Maultway Cl CBLY GU15 ....14 D3
Maultway Crs CBLY GU15 ....14 D3
Maultway North CBLY GU15 ....14 D5
The Maultway CBLY GU15 ....14 D5
CBLY GU15 ....23 F2
Mavins Rd FNM GU9 ....5 J7
Maxine Cl SHST GU47 ....11 H2
Maybrick Cl SHST GU47 ....11 F2
Maybury Cl FARN GU14 ....29 H1
May Cl SHST GU47 ....12 B5
May Crs ASHV GU12 ....50 A1
Mayfield RFNM GU10 ....60 B5
Mayfield Cl FNM GU9 ....49 F4
Mayfield Rd CBLY GU15 * 21 F5
FARN GU14 ....28 D2
Mayflower Dr YTLY GU46 ....10 A4
Maywood Dr CBLY GU15 ....14 D4
McGrigor Barracks ALDT GU11 ....43 F4
McKay Cl ALDT GU11 ....3 F1
Mc Naughton Cl FARN GU14 * 37 E1
Mead La FNM GU9 ....4 E4
Meadow Bank FNM GU9 ....4 E5
Meadowbank Rd LTWR GU18 ....16 C2
Meadow Cl ASHV GU12 ....39 F3
BLKW GU17 ....20 B2
Meadow Gate Av FARN GU14 ....37 H2
Meadow Rd FARN GU14 ....29 F2
Meadow Vw FLEETS GU52 ....40 A2
BLKW GU17 ....20 A1
FARN GU14 ....17 F5
RFNM GU10 ....60 B5
The Mead FARN GU14 * 38 B1
Meadway FRIM GU16 ....22 B4
Medlar Dr BLKW GU17 ....20 D3
Medows Cl FLEETN GU51 ....35 H4
Medway Dr FARN GU14 ....28 C2
Mellersh Cl FARN GU14 ....28 A4
Melrose Av FARN GU14 ....28 A4
Melville Av FRIM GU16 ....22 A3
Melville Ter FNM GU9 ....4 E4
Membury Cl FRIM GU16 ....30 C2
Mendip Rd FARN GU14 ....28 C2
Menin Wy FARN GU14 ....5 K6
Meon Cl FARN GU14 ....28 B3
Merivale FLEETS GU51 ....34 D4
Merlin Rd FARN GU14 ....38 B2
Merlins Cl FNM GU9 ....5 C6
Merlin Wy FARN GU14 ....37 F1
Merron Cl YTLY GU46 ....18 C1
Merryman Dr CWTH RG45 ....6 B2
Merrywood Pk CBLY GU15 ....22 B2
Merton Cl SHST GU47 ....12 D1
Meteor Wy FARN GU14 ....38 A3
Meudon Av FARN GU14 ....38 B1
Michaelmas Cl YTLY GU46 ....18 D2
Michelet Cl LTWR GU18 ....16 B2
Mickle HI SHST GU47 ....11 G2
Middle Av FNM GU9 ....54 B5
Middle Bourne La RFNM GU10 ....60 D2
Middle Church La FNM GU9 ....5 F4
Middle Cl CBLY GU15 ....14 D3
Middlefield FNM GU9 ....60 C1
Middlefield Cl FNM GU9 ....53 G5
Middle Gordon Rd CBLY GU15 ....21 C1
Middle HI ALDT GU11 ....2 D1
Middlemoor Rd FRIM GU16 ....30 A4
Middle Old Pk FNM GU9 ....53 F1
Middleton Gdns FARN GU14 ....28 C5
Middleton Rd CBLY GU15 ....14 A5
Mike Hawthorn Dr FNM GU9 ....5 H2
Milden Cl FRIM GU16 ....30 C3
Milden Gdns FRIM GU16 ....30 C3
Miles Pl LTWR GU18 ....15 H3
Miles Rd ASHV GU12 ....44 C5
Millbridge Rd YTLY GU46 ....10 B3
Mill Cl BAGS GU19 ....8 B5
Mill Cnr FLEETN GU51 ....27 E4

Mill Fld BAGS GU19 ....8 B5
Millins Cl SHST GU47 ....12 B2
Mill La RFNM GU10 ....62 D4
YTLY GU46 ....10 D4
Millmere YTLY GU46 ....10 D4
Mill Pond Rd BFOR GU20 ....9 G5
Mill Stream FARN GU14 ....48 C4
Minehurst Rd FRIM GU16 ....30 B5
Minerva Rd FARN GU14 ....38 B5
Minley Cl FARN GU14 ....28 B5
Minley Gv FLEETN GU51 ....35 H1
Minley Rd FARN GU14 ....19 E5
FARN GU14 ....28 A4
FLEETN GU51 ....26 D5
Minorca Av FRIM GU16 ....21 C4
Minorca Rd FRIM GU16 ....21 C5
Minstead Dr YTLY GU46 ....18 C1
Minster Ct CBLY GU15 * 20 D1
Mistletoe Rd YTLY GU46 ....18 D2
Mitcham Rd CBLY GU15 ....14 C2
Moffatts Cl SHST GU47 ....11 C3
Mole Cl FARN GU14 ....28 B3
Molyneux Rd BFOR GU20 ....9 G4
Monks Cl FARN GU14 ....28 B3
Monkshanger FNM GU9 ....54 C3
Monks Ri FLEETN GU51 ....34 C5
Monk's Wk RFNM GU10 ....61 H1
Monks' Well RFNM GU10 ....55 G5
Monkton La FARN GU14 ....28 B3
Mons Barracks ALDT GU11 ....43 G2
Mons Cl ALDT GU11 ....2 D5
Montacute Cl FARN GU14 ....29 H5
Montague Cl CBLY GU15 ....21 F1
LTWR GU18 ....16 A2
Montague La YTLY GU46 ....10 A5
Montgomery Ct SHST GU47 ....11 H3
Montgomery Rd FARN GU14 ....37 H1
Montrose Cl FLEETN GU51 ....35 H4
FRIM GU16 ....22 A4
Moons HI RFNM GU10 ....62 D1
Moor Cl SHST GU47 ....12 B2
Moore Cl FLEETS GU52 ....40 C2
RFNM GU10 ....50 B2
Moore Rd CHOB/PIR GU24 ....32 B3
FLEETS GU52 ....40 C2
Moorlands Cl FLEETN GU51 ....35 H4
Moorlands Rd CBLY GU15 ....21 E2
Moor Park La FNM GU9 ....54 C2
Moor Park Wy FNM GU9 ....54 D3
Moors Cl RFNM GU10 ....61 J4
Moor Pk BFOR GU20 ....9 F3
Moor Rd FARN GU14 ....29 E1
FRIM GU16 ....30 B1
Moorside Cl FARN GU14 ....29 E5
The Moors RFNM GU10 ....50 B5
Moray Av SHST GU47 ....12 B4
Mordaunt Dr CWTH RG45 ....6 A3
Moreton Cl FLEETS GU52 ....40 B3
Morland Rd ALDT GU11 ....49 G3
Morland's Rd ALDT GU11 ....43 H2
Morley Cl YTLY GU46 ....18 B1
Morley Rd FNM GU9 ....5 H6
Morris Rd FARN GU14 ....38 D4
Morton Cl FRIM GU16 ....30 B2
Morval Cl FARN GU14 ....28 C5
Moselle Cl FARN GU14 ....28 B4
Moulsham Copse La
CBLY GU15 ....10 B4
Moulsham La YTLY GU46 ....10 A5
Mountbatten Ri SHST GU47 ....11 F2
Mount Pleasant FNM GU9 ....4 C4
RGUW GU3 ....4 C4
SHST GU47 ....11 C2
Mount Pleasant Cl LTWR GU18 ....16 A2
Mount Pleasant Rd ASHV GU12 ....3 C5
Mounts Wy FLEETN GU51 ....34 C1
The Mount FLEETN GU51 ....34 C1
Mount Vw ALDT GU11 ....2 C5
Mulberry Cl ASHV GU12 ....44 C5
CWTH RG45 ....7 E4
SHST GU47 ....12 B5
Mulgrave Rd FRIM GU16 ....22 B2
Mulroy Dr CBLY GU15 ....14 C5
Munnings Dr SHST GU47 ....12 B5
Murray's La FARN GU14 ....37 H1
Murrell Rd ASHV GU12 ....44 B4
Murrells La CBLY GU15 ....21 F5
Myers Wy FRIM GU16 ....23 F4
Myrtle Cl LTWR GU18 ....16 B3
Myrtle Dr BLKW GU17 ....20 B2
Mytchett Farm Pk
FRIM GU16 ....39 F2
Mytchett Heath FRIM GU16 ....39 G3
Mytchett Lake Rd FRIM GU16 ....39 G5
Mytchett Place Rd FRIM GU16 ....39 G5
Mytchett Rd FRIM GU16 ....30 B5

N

Nairn Cl FRIM GU16 ....22 A4
Napier Cl ALDT GU11 ....39 E5
CWTH RG45 ....7 F4
Napier Dr CBLY GU15 ....14 C4
Napier Rd CWTH RG45 ....7 F4
Napoleon Av FARN GU14 ....28 D5
Nash Cl FARN GU14 ....28 D5
Nasturtium Dr CHOB/PIR GU24 ....25 C2
Neath Gdns FARN GU14 * 29 H5
FNM GU9 ....48 B2
Nelson Cl ASHV GU12 ....44 B5
Nelson Rd FNM GU9 ....48 B2
Nelson St ALDT GU11 ....2 D4
Nelson Wy CBLY GU15 ....20 D2
Netherhouse Moor
FLEETN GU51 ....34 C5
Nether Vell-Mead FLEETS GU52 ....40 A4
Netley St FARN GU14 ....38 C4
Nevada Cl FARN GU14 ....37 F1
Neville Duke Rd FARN GU14 ....28 C5
New Acres EWKG RG40 * 6 J1
Newark Rd BFOR GU20 ....9 E5
BLKW GU17 ....19 E5
New Barn Cl FLEETN GU51 ....34 B5
Newcome Pl ASHV GU12 ....49 H3

Newcome Rd FNM GU9 ....48 C3
New Dawn Cl FARN GU14 ....37 F1
Newfield Av FARN GU14 ....28 C3
Newfield Rd ASHV GU12 ....44 D3
Newfoundland Rd FRIM GU16 ....31 F1
Newlands FLEETS GU52 ....40 C1
Newlands Cl YTLY GU46 ....18 D1
Newlands Dr ASHV GU12 ....44 D3
Newlands Rd FRIM GU16 ....21 E5
Newmans Ct FNM GU9 ....53 F1
Newport Rd ALDT GU11 ....2 D5
New Rd BAGS GU19 ....8 D5
BLKW GU17 ....20 C2
CWTH RG45 ....7 E5
FLEETS GU52 ....34 A4
RFNM GU10 ....50 B4
SHST GU47 ....11 G3
Newton Rd FARN GU14 ....29 H3
Newton Wy RFNM GU10 ....50 A3
Newtown Rd SHST GU47 ....11 H5
New Wokingham Rd
CWTH RG45 ....6 C2
Nexus Pk ASHV GU12 ....39 F4
Nightingale Cl FARN GU14 ....28 A3
Nightingale Dr FRIM GU16 ....39 G1
Nightingale Gdns SHST GU47 ....11 H3
Nightingale Rd ASHV GU12 ....45 E4
Nightjar Cl RFNM GU10 ....46 D2
Nine Mile Ride EWKG RG40 ....6 A1
Norris Br FARN GU14 ....28 C4
Norris Hill Rd FLEETS GU52 ....36 B5
North Av FNM GU9 ....48 B3
Northbrook Rd ALDT GU11 ....2 C2
Northi Cl ASHV GU12 ....3 K5
FARN GU14 ....29 E1
Northcote Rd ASHV GU12 ....39 G5
FARN GU14 ....38 A1
North Downs Wy RFNM GU10 ....55 E3
RGUW GU3 ....57 G5
North Dr CHOB/PIR GU24 ....28 C2
North Farm Rd FARN GU14 ....28 C1
Northfield LTWR GU18 ....16 B3
Northfield Rd ASHV GU12 ....3 K4
Normandy Cl FRIM GU16 ....31 G1
Northfield Rd FLEETS GU52 ....40 D1
North Fryerne YTLY GU46 ....10 D3
Northgate Dr CBLY GU15 ....14 C4
North Gate Rd FARN GU14 ....38 B2
Northlands Cl ALDT GU11 ....3 J1
Northmead Farm FARN GU14 ....29 H5
North Rd ALDT GU11 ....38 D5
ASHV GU12 ....44 B3
North Side RFNM GU10 ....50 C5
Norton Rd CBLY GU15 ....23 E2
Norwich Av CBLY GU15 ....13 H6
Nuffield Dr SHST GU47 ....12 D2
Nugee Ct CWTH RG45 ....7 F4
Nursery Cl FLEETN GU51 ....36 B4
FRIM GU16 ....30 B2
Nutbourne FNM GU9 ....48 D3
Nuthatch Cl RFNM GU10 ....46 C3
Nutley Cl YTLY GU46 ....18 D1
Nutmeg Cl FARN GU14 ....24 A4
Nutshell La FNM GU9 ....48 A4

O

Oak Av CHOB/PIR GU24 ....33 G3
SHST GU47 ....12 B2
Oak Ct FNM GU9 ....5 F6
Oaken Copse CBLY GU15 ....15 E4
FLEETS GU52 ....40 C3
Oaken Copse Crs FARN GU14 ....29 F2
Oak Farm Cl BLKW GU17 ....20 A1
Oakfield Pl ALDT GU11 ....20 C2
Oakfield Rd BLKW GU17 ....20 C2
Oak Grove Crs CBLY GU15 ....12 D5
Oakland Av FNM GU9 ....48 C3
Oaklands YTLY GU46 ....10 C5
Oaklands La CWTH RG45 ....6 A2
Oaklea ASHV GU12 ....44 C2
Oakley Dr FLEETN GU51 ....35 G4
Oakley Rd CBLY GU15 ....21 F1
Oakridge CHOB/PIR GU24 ....17 F5
Oak Rd FARN GU14 ....38 C1
The Oaks FLEETS GU52 ....34 D3
YTLY GU46 ....18 D1
Oak Tree Cl ALDT GU11 ....3 K7
ASHV GU12 ....59 F5
WOKN/KNAP GU21 ....25 H5
Oak Tree Rd
WOKN/KNAP GU21 ....25 H5
Oaktrees ASHV GU12 ....50 B1
Oak Tree Vw FNM GU9 ....48 B4
Oaktree Wy SHST GU47 ....11 G2
Oakway RFNM GU10 ....58 A4
Oakway Dr FRIM GU16 ....22 A5
Oakwood FLEETS GU52 ....40 C3
Oakwood Ct CHOB/PIR GU24 ....25 C3
Oakwood Gdns
WOKN/KNAP GU21 ....25 G5
Oasthouse Dr FLEETN GU51 ....27 E5
Oast House La FNM GU9 ....48 B5
Oast La ALDT GU11 ....49 G3
Oatsheaf Pde FLEETN GU51 * 35 H4
Obelisk Wy CBLY GU15 ....21 F1
Oberursel Wy ALDT GU11 ....2 B1
O'Connor Rd ALDT GU11 ....38 D5
Odiham Rd RFNM GU10 ....46 B2
O'Gorman Av FARN GU14 ....28 B3
Okingham Ct SHST GU47 ....12 B2
Oldacre CHOB/PIR GU24 ....17 F4
Old Bisley Rd FRIM GU16 ....22 C4
Old Brickfield Rd ALDT GU11 ....49 F5
Oldbury Cl FRIM GU16 ....30 B2
Old Chapel La ASHV GU12 ....44 C5
Old Church La FNM GU9 ....61 F1
Old Compton La FNM GU9 ....54 B2
Oldcorne Hollow HTWY RG27 ....18 A1

Old Cove Rd FLEETN GU51 ....35 H1
Old Cross Tree Wy ASHV GU12 ....51 E2
Old Dean Rd CBLY GU15 ....13 H4
Olde Farm Dr BLKW GU17 ....19 H1
Old Farm Pl ASHV GU12 ....44 B3
Old Farnham La FNM GU9 ....5 H7
RFNM GU10 ....52 A4
Old Forge End SHST GU47 ....11 H4
Old Frensham Rd RFNM GU10 ....61 F2
Old Green La CBLY GU15 ....13 G4
Old Guildford Rd FRIM GU16 ....30 D4
Old Heath Wy FARN GU14 ....48 A3
Oldhouse La CHOB/PIR GU24 ....16 C1
CHOB/PIR GU24 ....25 C1
Old La ALDT GU11 ....44 A4
ASHV GU12 ....44 A4
The Old Orch FNM GU9 ....53 F5
Old Park Cl FNM GU9 ....47 G4
Old Park Rd FNM GU9 ....47 F3
Old Pasture Rd FRIM GU16 ....22 B3
Old Pharmacy Ct CWTH RG45 * 7 E4
Old Pond Cl FRIM GU16 ....21 F5
Old Portsmouth Rd CBLY GU15 ....22 C2
Old Pumphouse Cl
FLEETN GU51 ....35 H2
Old Rectory Dr ASHV GU12 ....44 D5
Old Rectory Gdns FARN GU14 ....29 H5
Old Sawmill La CWTH RG45 ....7 E2
Old School Cl ASHV GU12 ....44 C4
FARN GU14 ....29 E5
Old School La YTLY GU46 ....10 C5
Old Town Ms FNM GU9 * 4 D4
Old Welmore YTLY GU46 ....19 E1
Old Wokingham Rd CWTH RG45 ....7 F1
Oleander Cl CWTH RG45 ....6 B1
Orchard Cl FARN GU14 ....44 C2
CHOB/PIR GU24 ....16 D5
FARN GU14 ....20 D5
FNM GU9 ....48 A4
Orchard End RFNM GU10 ....60 B5
Orchard Gdns ALDT GU11 ....3 H7
Orchard Ga SHST GU47 ....11 H3
Orchard HI BFOR GU20 ....9 H5
Orchard La FARN GU14 ....29 E5
FNM GU9 ....48 A4
The Orchard LTWR GU18 ....16 B3
Orchard Wy ALDT GU11 ....3 H7
CBLY GU15 ....21 F4
Orchid Dr CHOB/PIR GU24 ....25 C2
Ordnance Rd ALDT GU11 ....3 J1
Oriel HI CBLY GU15 ....21 H2
Orwell Cl FARN GU14 ....28 C2
Osborne Dr FLEETS GU52 ....35 H5
LTWR GU18 ....16 A3
Osborne Rd FARN GU14 ....38 C4
Osborn Rd FNM GU9 ....54 B1
Osnaburgh HI CBLY GU15 ....21 F1
Osprey Gdns ALDT GU11 ....49 E3
Otter Cl CWTH RG45 ....6 C1
Overdale HI FRIM GU16 ....22 C3
Overlord Cl CBLY GU15 ....13 J5
Overton Cl ALDT GU11 ....49 G4
Owen Rd BFOR GU20 ....9 H3
Owlsmoor Rd SHST GU47 ....12 B3
Oxenden Ct RFNM GU10 ....50 A2
Oxenden Rd RFNM GU10 ....50 A2
Oxford Rd FARN GU14 ....38 C3
SHST GU47 ....12 C1

P

Packway FNM GU9 ....61 F1
Paddock Cl CBLY GU15 ....14 C5
The Paddock CWTH RG45 ....6 C7
RFNM GU10 * 60 B4
Paget Cl CBLY GU15 ....14 D4
Pakenham Dr ALDT GU11 ....2 C1
Pale La HTWY RG27 ....26 A4
HTWY RG27 ....34 A1
Palmerston Ct FARN GU14 ....37 F2
Pannells RFNM GU10 ....61 F3
Pan's Gdns CBLY GU15 ....22 B2
The Parade ASHV GU12 * 44 C3
FRIM GU16 * 29 H1
Parfitts Cl FNM GU9 ....53 E5
Parish Cl ASHV GU12 ....50 D1
FNM GU9 ....47 G4
Parish Rd FARN GU14 ....38 B4
Park Av CBLY GU15 ....21 G2
Park Barn YTLY GU46 ....18 C1
Park HI FLEETS GU52 ....40 B3
Parkhill Cl BLKW GU17 ....20 B2
Parkhill Rd BLKW GU17 ....20 B2
Parkland Gv FNM GU9 ....2 A7
Park La ALDT GU11 ....3 F1
Park HI FLEETS GU52 ....21 C1
Park Rd ALDT GU11 ....3 F7
CBLY GU15 ....21 C1
FARN GU14 ....39 E3
FNM GU9 ....47 G4
SHST GU47 ....12 A4
Park Rw FNM GU9 ....5 F2
Parkside FNM GU9 ....48 A4
Parkstone Dr CBLY GU15 ....21 G2
Park St BAGS GU19 ....8 C5
Park Vw BAGS GU19 ....8 B5
Parkway CBLY GU15 ....21 C3
CWTH RG45 ....6 C3
Parliamentary Rd
CHOB/PIR GU24 ....32 A3
Parnham Av LTWR GU18 ....16 D3
Parsonage Wy FRIM GU16 ....22 A5
Parsons Cl FLEETS GU52 ....40 B2
Parsons Fld SHST GU47 ....11 H3
Partridge Av YTLY GU46 ....10 D5
Partridge Cl FRIM GU16 ....39 G2
RFNM GU10 ....46 D2
Paschal Rd CBLY GU15 ....14 B3
Paterson Cl FRIM GU16 ....23 E3
The Pathfinders FARN GU14 ....37 E1

Patten Av YTLY GU46 ....18 C1
Paul Cl ALDT GU11 ....48 C2
Pavillion Rd ALDT GU11 ....42 A1
  ALDT GU11 ....48 C1
The Pavilions End CBLY GU15 ....21 H3
Pawley Cl RFNM GU10 ....50 B3
Pawmers Md FLEETS GU52 ....40 A4
Peabody Rd FARN GU14 ....38 D5
Peach Tree Cl FARN GU14 ....39 E2
Peakfield RFNM GU10 ....63 E4
Pear Tree Av FLEETN GU51 ....15 E3
Pear Tree La RFNM GU10 ....60 B5
Peat Moor Cl FLEETS GU51 ....35 E2
Peatmoor Cl FLEETN GU51 ....35 E2
Peatmore Dr CHOB/PIR GU24 ....32 C3
Peddlars Gv YTLY GU46 ....11 E5
Peel Av FRIM GU16 ....30 C2
Pegasus Av ASHV GU12 ....44 A4
Pegasus Rd FARN GU14 * 38 B2
  FARN GU14 ....38 B2
Peggotty Pl SHST GU47 ....12 C1
Pelham Pl RFNM GU10 ....60 C4
Pembroke Broadway
  CBLY GU15 ....21 G3
Pembury Pl ASHV GU12 ....3 G5
Pendragon Wy CBLY GU15 ....23 F2
Penfold Cft FNM GU9 ....54 D1
Pengilly Rd FNM GU9 ....54 D1
Peninsular Cl CBLY GU15 ....14 D4
Pennefather's Rd ALDT GU11 ....42 D4
Pennine Wy FARN GU14 ....28 C2
Penns Wd FARN GU14 ....38 D5
Penns Yd FNM GU9 ....54 D1
Pennypot La CHOB/PIR GU24 ....17 H5
Penrhyn Cl ALDT GU11 ....2 E5
Pensford Cl CWTH RG45 ....6 D1
Penshurst Ri FRIM GU16 ....30 B1
Percheron Dr
  WOKN/KNAP GU21 ....33 H3
Perowne St ALDT GU11 ....42 D4
Perring Av FARN GU14 ....28 C1
Perring Rd FARN GU14 ....38 A3
Perry Dr FLEETN GU51 ....55 F4
Perryhill Cft SHST GU47 ....11 F2
Perry Hill FNM GU9 ....47 H5
  LTWR GU18 ....15 H4
Peterhouse Cl SHST GU47 ....12 D1
Petworth Cl FRIM GU16 ....30 D1
Pevensey Wy FRIM GU16 ....30 C1
Pheasant Copse FLEETN GU51 ....14 D2
Phillips Cl RFNM GU10 ....50 A2
Pickford St ALDT GU11 ....2 E3
Pickwick Gdns CBLY GU15 ....22 D2
Picton St FLEETN GU51 ....15 E4
Pierrefondes Av FARN GU14 ....29 F4
Pike Cl ALDT GU11 ....3 H2
Pilgrims Cl FNM GU9 ....4 D7
Pilgrims Vw ASHV GU12 ....51 E2
Pilgrims Wy CHOB/PIR GU24 ....25 G3
Pine Av CBLY GU15 ....21 H3
  CHOB/PIR GU24 ....25 G2
Pine Cl ASHV GU12 ....44 C1
  CBLY GU15 ....13 G4
Pine Ct FRIM GU16 * 39 C4
Pine Dr BLKW GU17 ....20 C5
Pinefields Cft CWTH RG45 ....5 H5
Pine Gv BFOR GU20 ....9 H4
  FLEETS GU52 ....40 D2
  RFNM GU10 ....61 G2
Pinehurst Ri SHST GU47 ....11 H5
Pinehill Rd CWTH RG45 ....6 D4
Pinehurst Av FARN GU14 ....38 B2
Pinehurst Rd FARN GU14 ....38 A2
Pine Mount Rd CBLY GU15 ....21 H2
Pine Ridge Dr RFNM GU10 ....60 D5
Pines Rd FLEETN GU51 ....15 E4
The Pines CBLY GU15 ....14 B4
Pine View Cl FNM GU9 ....49 E5
Pinewood Av CWTH RG45 ....6 D2
Pinewood Cl SHST GU47 ....11 F1
Pinewood Crs FARN GU14 ....28 A5
Pinewood Gdns BAGS GU19 ....38 A5
Pinewood Hi FLEETN GU51 ....35 G2
Pinewood Pk FARN GU14 ....28 B2
Pinewood Rd ASHV GU12 ....45 F4
Pipers Cft FLEETS GU52 ....40 D5
Pipers Patch FARN GU14 ....29 F5
Pipsons Cl YTLY GU46 ....11 F5
Pirbright Rd FARN GU14 ....38 C1
  RGUW GU3 ....45 H3
Pirbright Ter CHOB/PIR GU24 * 33 F5
Pitt La ALDT GU11 ....62 C5
Pitt Wy FARN GU14 ....28 D4
Plough Rd YTLY GU46 ....11 F5
Plovers Rd CHOB/PIR GU24 ....33 E2
Polden Cl FARN GU14 ....28 C2
Polkerris Wy FLEETS GU52 ....40 D5
Pollard Gv CBLY GU15 ....23 G2
Polmear Cl FLEETS GU52 ....40 D5
Pond Cft YTLY GU46 ....11 E5
Pond Rd FARN GU14 ....38 B2
Pondtail Cl FLEETN GU51 ....36 A4
Pondtail Gdns FLEETN GU51 ....36 A4
Pondtail Rd FLEETN GU51 ....36 A4
Pondview Cl FLEETN GU51 ....36 A2
Pool Rd ALDT GU11 ....49 G3
Poplar Av BFOR GU20 ....9 E2
Poplar Cl FRIM GU16 ....39 G1
Poplars Cl FARN GU14 ....28 A4
Poplar Wk FNM GU9 ....48 B5
Poppyhills Rd CBLY GU15 ....14 B5
Portesbery Rd CBLY GU15 ....13 H5
Portesbery Hill Dr CBLY GU15 ....13 H4
Portland Dr FLEETS GU52 ....40 B5
Portland Ter FNM GU9 * 54 B1
Portsmouth Rd FRIM GU16 ....22 A3
Port Wy CHOB/PIR GU24 ....25 G4
Potley Hill Rd YTLY GU46 ....19 F1
Potteries La FRIM GU16 ....39 F1
The Potteries FARN GU14 ....28 B5
Potters Crs ASHV GU12 ....44 D4
Potters Ga FNM GU9 ....4 D3
Pottery La RFNM GU10 ....60 B3
Pound Farm La ASHV GU12 ....51 F1
Pound La BFOR GU20 ....9 G4

Pound Rd ASHV GU12 ....3 F4
Poyle Rd RFNM GU10 ....50 C3
Prentice Cl FARN GU14 ....29 F1
Priest La CHOB/PIR GU24 ....24 C2
Primrose Dr CHOB/PIR GU24 ....25 G2
Primrose Gdns FARN GU14 ....37 G1
Primrose Wy SHST GU47 ....11 H2
Prince Charles Crs FARN GU14 ....39 F3
Prince Dr SHST GU47 ....11 G2
Prince's Av ALDT GU11 ....43 G2
Princes Cl BAGS GU19 ....15 G5
Princess Wy CBLY GU15 ....21 G1
Princes Wy ALDT GU11 ....2 C2
Prior Croft Cl CBLY GU15 ....22 D2
Prior End CBLY GU15 ....22 C1
Prior Rd CBLY GU15 ....22 C1
Priors Cl FARN GU14 ....29 F1
Priors Keep FLEETS GU52 ....35 H4
Prior's La BLKW GU17 ....19 G1
Priory Cl FLEETN GU51 ....34 D4
Priory Ct CBLY GU15 * 20 D1
Priory La RFNM GU10 ....63 F3
Priory St FARN GU14 ....29 H5
Propeller Rd FARN GU14 ....37 E1
Prospect Av FARN GU14 ....29 F5
Prospect Rd ASHV GU12 ....44 B1
  FARN GU14 ....29 E5
  RFNM GU10 ....60 B5
Prunus Cl CHOB/PIR GU24 ....17 E5
Puckridge Gate Rd ALDT GU11 ....42 B1
Puckridge Hill Rd ALDT GU11 ....42 C2
Purcell Rd CWTH RG45 ....6 D1
Purley Wy FRIM GU16 ....30 A1
Purmerend Cl FARN GU14 ....28 A4
Puttenham Rd RFNM GU10 ....56 D1
Pyestock Crs FARN GU14 ....27 H5

Q

The Quadrangle FARN GU14 * 29 G3
The Quadrant ASHV GU12 ....44 A3
Quarry Bank LTWR GU18 ....15 H5
Quarry La YTLY GU46 ....19 E1
Quarters Rd FARN GU14 ....38 D2
Quebec Gdns BLKW GU17 ....37 G1
Queen Anne's Ga FNM GU9 ....48 B3
Queen Elizabeth Cl ASHV GU12 ....44 C5
Queen Elizabeth Dr ALDT GU11 ....2 B3
Queen Elizabeth Rd
  CBLY GU15 ....13 H2
Queen Mary Av CBLY GU15 ....21 E1
Queen Mary Rd ALDT GU11 ....42 D5
Queen's Av ALDT GU11 ....43 F2
Queensbury Pl BLKW GU17 ....20 A3
Queens Cl CHOB/PIR GU24 ....25 G4
  FARN GU14 ....38 B4
Queens Ct FNM GU9 ....4 A7
Queen's Gate Rd FARN GU14 ....38 B5
Queens La FNM GU9 ....47 H3
Queensmead FARN GU14 ....38 B1
Queens Ride CWTH RG45 ....6 C1
Queens Rd ALDT GU11 ....2 B5
  CBLY GU15 ....21 F2
  FARN GU14 ....38 B4
  FLEETS GU52 ....35 G5
  FNM GU9 ....48 A4
Queen St ASHV GU12 ....3 G4
Queensway FRIM GU16 ....30 C2
Quennells Hi RFNM GU10 ....60 A2
Quince Dr CHOB/PIR GU24 ....25 H2

R

Rackstraw Rd SHST GU47 ....12 B2
Radar Rd FARN GU14 ....37 F3
Radcliffe Cl FRIM GU16 ....30 C1
Radford Cl FNM GU9 ....48 C5
Rae Rd FARN GU14 ....38 B5
Raeburn Wy SHST GU47 ....12 B3
RAF Gate Rd FARN GU14 ....37 G1
Raglan Cl ASHV GU12 ....44 C5
  FRIM GU16 ....30 D1
Raleigh Wy CBLY GU15 ....22 D3
Ramillies Cl ALDT GU11 ....39 E5
Ramsay Cl CBLY GU15 ....14 D3
Ramsdell Rd FLEETN GU51 ....54 D1
Randolph Dr FARN GU14 ....37 E1
Range Ride CBLY GU15 ....13 G4
Range Rd FARN GU14 ....37 F2
Range Vw SHST GU47 ....12 B2
Rankine Cl FNM GU9 ....49 E4
Rapallo Cl FNM GU9 ....49 E4
Rapley Cl CBLY GU15 ....14 B3
Rapley's Fld CHOB/PIR GU24 ....33 E5
Rapsley La WOKN/KNAP GU21 ....25 H5
Rashleigh Ct FLEETS GU52 ....35 F1
Rasset Md FARN GU14 ....40 A4
Ratcliffe Rd FARN GU14 ....28 C1
Raven Cl YTLY GU46 ....11 E5
Ravenscroft Cl ASHV GU12 ....44 B5
Ravenstone Rd CBLY GU15 ....23 F1
Ravenswood Av CWTH RG45 ....6 A3
Ravenswood Dr CBLY GU15 ....22 C1
Rawlinson Rd ALDT GU11 ....42 D5
  CBLY GU15 ....12 D5
Raygnoldes FLEETS GU52 ....40 A4
Reading Rd BLKW GU17 ....19 H2
  FARN GU14 ....38 C3
  YTLY GU46 ....10 A4
Reading Rd North
  FLEETN GU51 ....34 D2
Reading Rd South
  FLEETN GU51 ....34 D3
Rebecca Cl FLEETS GU52 ....40 A4
Recreation Cl FARN GU14 ....20 D5
Recreation Rd RFNM GU10 ....60 A5
Rectory Cl SHST GU47 ....11 F3
Rectory La BFOR GU20 ....9 G5

RFNM GU10 ....58 B4
Rectory Rd FARN GU14 ....29 G5
Redan Gdns ASHV GU12 ....3 F3
Redan Hill Est ASHV GU12 * 3 H3
Redan Rd ASHV GU12 ....3 G3
Redcrest Gdns CBLY GU15 ....22 B1
Redfields La FLEETS GU52 ....46 A1
Redlands La RFNM GU10 ....46 A3
Red Lion La FNM GU9 ....3 F6
Redmayne CBLY GU15 ....23 F2
Red Oaks RFNM GU10 * 60 A5
Red Rd LTWR GU18 ....16 A4
Redvers Buller Rd ALDT GU11 ....38 C5
Redwood Dr CBLY GU15 ....23 F2
Redwoods Wy FLEETS GU52 ....35 H4
Reed Cl ALDT GU11 ....3 H2
The Reeds Rd RFNM GU10 ....63 F2
Reeves Rd ASHV GU12 ....3 G4
Regent Cl FLEETN GU51 ....35 G4
Regent St BAGS GU19 ....15 H1
Regents Pl SHST GU47 ....12 A3
Regent St FLEETN GU51 ....35 G4
Regent Wy FRIM GU16 ....22 B5
Regiment Cl FARN GU14 ....37 E1
Reservoir Rd FARN GU14 ....37 F1
Revelstoke Av FARN GU14 ....29 E4
Revesby Cl CHOB/PIR GU24 ....16 D5
Rhododendron Rd FRIM GU16 ....30 D1
Ribble Pl FARN GU14 ....30 A1
Richard Cl FLEETN GU51 ....35 E5
Richards Cl ASHV GU12 * 44 C2
Richmond Cl FARN GU14 ....37 F1
  FLEETS GU52 ....40 C4
  FRIM GU16 ....22 B5
Richmond Rd SHST GU47 ....12 C4
Rideway Cl CBLY GU15 ....21 F2
Ridgeway Cl LTWR GU18 ....16 A3
The Ridgeway CHOB/PIR GU24 ....33 F2
  LTWR GU18 ....16 B2
Ridgewood Dr FRIM GU16 ....30 D1
Ridgway Hill Rd FNM GU9 ....54 A5
Ridgway Rd FNM GU9 ....54 A5
Ridgway Pde FNM GU9 * 54 A5
The Ridings FARN GU14 ....22 D3
Ridley Cl FLEETS GU52 ....35 F5
Rifle Wy FARN GU14 ....37 E1
Rimbault Cl ALDT GU11 ....38 D5
Ringwood Rd BLKW GU17 ....12 A5
  FARN GU14 ....29 G2
Ripon Cl FARN GU14 ....30 A1
Ripon Rd BLKW GU17 ....19 F5
Ripplesmore Cl SHST GU47 ....11 H5
The Rise CWTH RG45 ....6 B5
Riverdale RFNM GU10 ....60 A1
River La FNM GU9 ....60 A1
Rivermead Rd CBLY GU15 ....21 F4
River Rw YTLY GU46 ....10 B4
River Rw FNM GU9 ....53 F5
Rivers Ct FARN GU14 ....39 E3
Riverside Av LTWR GU18 ....16 C5
Riverside Cl CHOB/PIR GU24 ....33 F2
Riverside Wy CBLY GU15 ....21 E3
Robertson Wy ASHV GU12 ....50 B1
Roberts Rd ASHV GU12 ....3 J4
  CBLY GU15 ....13 E5
Robert Wy FRIM GU16 ....39 F1
Robin Cl ASHV GU12 ....44 B1
Robin Hill Dr CBLY GU15 ....22 C5
Robin Hood Cl FARN GU14 ....29 E2
Robin La SHST GU47 ....11 H2
Robins Grove Crs YTLY GU46 ....10 A5
Rochester Gv FLEETN GU51 ....35 F4
The Rockery FARN GU14 ....37 F3
Rocket Rd FARN GU14 ....37 F3
Rockfield Wy SHST GU47 * 12 B3
Rock Gdns ALDT GU11 ....2 A4
Rock La RFNM GU10 ....60 C3
Rodmel Ct FARN GU14 ....39 E3
Rokes Pl YTLY GU46 ....10 D5
Roman Wy FNM GU9 ....54 C1
The Romany FARN GU14 ....36 C3
Romayne Cl FARN GU14 ....29 E4
Romney Cl FARN GU14 ....37 G3
Romsey Cl ALDT GU11 ....49 G4
  BLKW GU17 ....37 G1
Rook Wk FLEETN GU51 ....35 F2
Rookwood Av SHST GU47 ....12 C2
Rorkes Drift FRIM GU16 ....30 B1
Rosary Gdns YTLY GU46 * 10 D5
Rosebury Dr CHOB/PIR GU24 ....25 G2
Rosedale ASHV GU12 ....3 G3
Rosedene Gdns FLEETS GU52 ....35 F2
Rosedene La SHST GU47 ....12 B4
Rose Gdns FARN GU14 ....37 F1
Rosemary Av ASHV GU12 ....39 G4
Rosemary Cl FARN GU14 ....28 B4
Rosemary Gdns FARN GU14 * 20 A1
Rosemary La BLKW GU17 ....37 G1
  RFNM GU10 ....60 A4
Rose Wk FLEETN GU51 ....35 F2
Rosewood Wy CHOB/PIR GU24 ....17 F5
Rosslea BFOR GU20 ....9 E2
Rossmore Gdns ALDT GU11 ....2 A3
Rother Cl SHST GU47 ....12 A3
Rother Rd FARN GU14 ....28 C3
Rotten Green Rd FLEETS GU52 ....26 A3
Rotunda Est ALDT GU11 * 2 A1
Rounce La CHOB/PIR GU24 ....16 D5
Roundway CBLY GU15 ....15 E5
Roundway Cl CBLY GU15 ....15 E5
Rounton Rd FLEETS GU52 ....35 H3
Rowan Cha RFNM GU10 ....60 C2
Rowan Cl CBLY GU15 ....14 B5
  FLEETN GU51 ....36 A3
Rowan Dl FLEETS GU52 ....40 A5
Rowan Dr CWTH RG45 ....7 E1
Rowans Cl FARN GU14 ....20 C5
Rowcroft Cl ASHV GU12 ....44 C1
Rowhill Av ALDT GU11 ....48 C3
Rowhill Crs ALDT GU11 ....2 A5
Rowhills FNM GU9 ....48 B2
Rowhills Cl FNM GU9 ....2 A7

Roxbee Cox Rd FARN GU14 ....36 C3
Roxburgh Cl CBLY GU15 ....23 E2
Royale Cl ALDT GU11 ....3 H7
Royal Oak Cl YTLY GU46 ....11 E5
Rubus Cl CHOB/PIR GU24 ....17 E5
Rudd Hall Ri CBLY GU15 ....21 H3
Rufford Cl FLEETS GU52 ....40 C1
Rugby Cl SHST GU47 ....12 C2
Rugosa Rd CHOB/PIR GU24 ....17 E5
Runwick La RFNM GU10 ....52 D4
Rushden Wy FNM GU9 ....48 B3
Rushmoor Cl FLEETS GU52 ....35 G5
Rushmoor Rd ALDT GU11 ....42 C4
Ruskin Ct CWTH RG45 * 6 B4
Russell Ct BLKW GU17 ....20 B1
Russet Cl RFNM GU10 ....50 A3
Russet Gdns CBLY GU15 ....21 H5
Russet Gld FNM GU9 ....48 B2
Russetts Dr FLEETS GU51 ....35 G4
Rustic Gln FLEETS GU52 ....40 B2
Ruth Cl FARN GU14 ....28 A4
Rutland Cl ALDT GU11 ....2 D1
Ryan Mt SHST GU47 ....11 G3
Rydal Cl CBLY GU15 ....23 F1
  FARN GU14 ....30 A1
Rydal Dr FLEETS GU52 ....40 A2
Rydal Pl LTWR GU18 ....16 B3
Ryebeck Rd FLEETS GU52 ....40 C2
Rye Cl FARN GU14 ....28 C3
  FLEETN GU51 ....27 E4
Rye Cft FLEETS GU52 ....40 A5
Rye Gv CHOB/PIR GU24 ....17 E2
Ryecroft Gdns BLKW GU17 ....20 C2
Ryeland Cl FLEETN GU51 * 27 E4
Ryelaw Rd FLEETS GU52 ....40 C2
Ryle Rd FNM GU9 ....4 E7
Ryves Av YTLY GU46 ....18 A1

S

Sabre Ct ALDT GU11 ....42 C5
Saddleback Rd CWTH RG45 ....11 H4
Saddleback Wy FLEETN GU51 ....36 D5
Saddler Cnr SHST GU47 ....11 H4
Saddlewood CBLY GU15 ....21 G2
Sagittarius CHOB/PIR GU24 * 11 H3
St Andrew Av CHOB/PIR GU24 ....33 H3
St Andrews Ct CWTH RG45 ....6 B2
St Andrew's Wy FRIM GU16 ....30 B2
St Annes Gld BAGS GU19 ....35 F5
St Augustine's Cl ASHV GU12 ....3 K4
St Barnabas Av
  ....33 G4
St Benedict's Cl ALDT GU11 ....2 C5
St Catherines Rd FRIM GU16 ....22 C5
St Christophers Cl ASHV GU12 ....3 J2
St Christophers Pl FARN GU14 * 37 H3
St Christopher's Rd
  ....38 A1
St Cross Rd FNM GU9 ....5 G2
  FRIM GU16 ....30 C2
St David's Cl FARN GU14 ....28 D1
St George Av CHOB/PIR GU24 ....33 H3
St George's Cl FARN GU9 * 49 F4
St Georges Ms FARN GU14 ....5 F2
St Georges Rd ASHV GU12 ....3 J5
  CBLY GU15 ....13 H5
  FARN GU14 ....38 C3
  FNM GU9 ....49 F5
  RFNM GU10 ....55 F1
St George's Rd East ASHV GU12 ....3 H7
St Georges Yd FNM GU9 * 4 D6
St Helens Crs SHST GU47 ....11 H3
St James' Av FNM GU9 ....54 C1
St James Rd FLEETN GU51 ....35 F4
St James' Ter FNM GU9 ....5 H1
St Johns Ct FARN GU14 * 28 B4
St Johns Gv FARN GU14 ....60 D1
St John's Rd FARN GU14 ....28 C5
  FNM GU9 ....53 H3
  SHST GU47 ....11 H4
St Joseph's Rd ALDT GU11 ....2 D5
St Mark Av CHOB/PIR GU24 ....33 H3
St Marks Cl FARN GU14 ....38 C3
St Marks Rd FNM GU9 * 47 A3
St Marks Cl SHST GU47 ....12 B3
St Mary's Gdns BAGS GU19 ....8 C5
St Mary's Rd ASHV GU12 ....44 C2
  CBLY GU15 ....13 G5
St Michaels Cl FLEETN GU51 ....36 A4
St Michael's Rd ALDT GU11 ....2 F1
  CBLY GU15 * 21 F1
  FARN GU14 ....29 F3
  SHST GU47 ....11 F3
St Nicholas Cl FLEETN GU51 ....35 F3
St Omer Barracks ALDT GU11 ....43 H2
St Pauls Cl RFNM GU10 ....50 B3
St Peter's Gdns RFNM GU10 ....60 B2
  YTLY GU46 ....10 D5
St Peters Md ASHV GU12 ....44 D5
St Peters Rk FNM GU9 ....48 C3
St Peter's Wy FRIM GU16 ....30 B2
St Saviour Av CHOB/PIR GU24 ....33 H3
Salamanca CWTH RG45 ....6 A3
Salerno Cl ALDT GU11 ....2 B3
Salesian Vw FARN GU14 ....38 C4
Salisbury Gv FRIM GU16 ....39 G1
Salisbury Rd ALDT GU11 ....44 C5
  BLKW GU17 ....29 C5
  FARN GU14 ....38 C3
Salisbury Ter FRIM GU16 ....39 G1
Saltram Rd FARN GU14 ....30 A1
Samarkand Cl CBLY GU15 ....22 D2
San Carlos Ap ALDT GU11 ....2 B3
Sandford Rd ALDT GU11 ....42 B3
  FNM GU9 ....47 H5
Sandhi Av YTLY GU46 ....29 F2
Sandhurst La BLKW GU17 ....19 F5
Sandhurst Rd CWTH RG45 ....6 D5
  YTLY GU46 ....11 E5
Sandown Cl BLKW GU17 ....20 B1
Sandown Crs ALDT GU11 ....49 F3

Sandown Dr FRIM GU16 ....2 ...
Sandringham Wy FRIM GU16 ....30 ...
Sandrock Hill Rd RFNM GU10 ....60 ...
Sands Ct FRIM GU16 ....55 ...
Sands Rd RFNM GU10 ....55 ...
Sandy Hill Rd FNM GU9 ....47 ...
Sandy La CBLY GU15 ....14 ...
  FARN GU14 ....28 ...
  FLEETS GU52 ....63 ...
  RFNM GU10 ....63 ...
  SHST GU47 ....11 ...
Sankey La FLEETN GU51 ....36 ...
Santina Cl FNM GU9 ....48 ...
Sarah Wy FARN GU14 ....29 ...
Saunton Gdns FARN GU14 ....29 ...
Saville Gdns CBLY GU15 ....22 ...
Savoy Gv BLKW GU17 ....20 ...
Saxon Cft FNM GU9 ....5 ...
Saxony Wy YTLY GU46 * ....19 ...
Sayers Cl FRIM GU16 ....30 ...
Sbac Tr ALDT GU11 ....42 ...
Scarlet Oaks CBLY GU15 ....21 ...
Scarlett's Rd ALDT GU11 ....43 ...
School Cl CHOB/PIR GU24 ....25 ...
School Hi CWTH RG45 ....6 ...
  RFNM GU10 ....56 ...
  RFNM GU10 ....50 ...
  SHST GU47 ....11 ...
School La BAGS GU19 ....15 ...
  BFOR GU20 ....9 ...
  CHOB/PIR GU24 ....33 ...
  RFNM GU10 ....58 ...
  RFNM GU10 ....60 ...
  RGUW GU3 ....45 ...
  YTLY GU46 ....10 ...
School Rd BFOR GU20 ....9 ...
  ....60 ...
Scotland Cl ASHV GU12 ....44 ...
Scotland Farm Rd ASHV GU12 ....44 ...
Scotland Hi SHST GU47 ....11 ...
Scott's Ct FARN GU14 ....29 ...
Scott's Grove Rd
  CHOB/PIR GU24 ....25 ...
Seafire Wy FARN GU14 ....37 ...
Seale La RFNM GU10 ....53 ...
  RGUW GU3 ....53 ...
Seale Rd MFD/CHID GU8 ....65 ...
Searle Rd FNM GU9 ....5 ...
Seaton Rd CBLY GU15 ....21 ...
Sebastopol Rd ALDT GU11 ....2 ...
Sedgemoor FARN GU14 ....28 ...
Seebys Oak SHST GU47 ....11 ...
Selborne Av ASHV GU12 ....44 ...
Selborne Av ALDT GU11 ....48 ...
Selborne Gdns FNM GU9 ....47 ...
Selborne Gdns FNM GU9 ....12 ...
Selwyn Dr YTLY GU46 ....18 ...
Sepen Meade FLEETS GU52 ....40 ...
The Sett YTLY GU46 ....2 ...
Severn Cl SHST GU47 ....12 ...
Severn Rd FARN GU14 ....30 ...
Seymour Dr CBLY GU15 ....15 ...
Shackleton Cl ASHV GU12 ....44 ...
Shady Nook FNM GU9 ....47 ...
Shaftesbury Mt BLKW GU17 ....20 ...
Shaftesbury Rd
  CHOB/PIR GU24 ....25 ...
Shakespeare Gdns FARN GU14 ....28 ...
Shalbourne Ri CBLY GU15 ....21 ...
Shalden Rd ASHV GU12 ....3 ...
Shaldon Wy FLEETN GU51 ....36 ...
Shamrock Cl FRIM GU16 ....30 ...
Shanklin Ct ASHV GU12 ....3 ...
Shawfield La ASHV GU12 ....44 ...
Shawfield Rd ASHV GU12 ....50 ...
Shaw Pk CWTH RG45 ....6 ...
Sheephouse FNM GU9 ....5 ...
Sheet's Heath La
  CHOB/PIR GU24 ....33 ...
Sheffield Cl FARN GU14 ....28 ...
Shelley Cl FLEETN GU51 ....28 ...
Shelley La RFNM GU10 ....51 ...
Shelley Wk YTLY GU46 ....18 ...
Shelly Ri FARN GU14 ....29 ...
Shepherd & Flock Roundabout
  RFNM GU10 ....54 ...
Shepherds Cha BAGS GU19 ....15 ...
Shepherds Wk FARN GU14 ....28 ...
Shepherds Vw CWTH RG45 ....7 ...
Sheraton Cl BLKW GU17 ....20 ...
Sherborne Rd FARN GU14 ....38 ...
Sheridan Cl ALDT GU11 ....2 ...
Sheridan Rd FRIM GU16 ....30 ...
Sherington Ct FARN GU14 ....38 ...
Sherwin Crs FARN GU14 ....37 ...
Shetland Wy FLEETN GU51 ....23 ...
Shildon Cl CBLY GU15 ....23 ...
Ship Aly FARN GU14 ....2 ...
Ship La FARN GU14 ....37 ...
Shire Av FLEETN GU51 ....23 ...
Shire Cl BAGS GU19 ....8 ...
Shires Wy YTLY GU46 ....11 ...
Shoe La ALDT GU11 ....1 ...
Short Dale Rd ALDT GU11 ....48 ...
Shortfield Rd RFNM GU10 ....60 ...
Shortheath Crest FNM GU9 ....60 ...
Shortheath Rd FNM GU9 ....60 ...
Short St ALDT GU11 ....1 ...
Shrubbery Cl SHST GU47 ....12 ...
The Shrubbery FARN GU14 ....29 ...
Shrubbs Rd RFNM GU10 ....60 ...
Shrublands Dr LTWR GU18 ....16 ...
Sian Cl FLEETS GU52 ....35 ...
Sidestrand Rd ALDT GU11 ....37 ...
The Sidings ALDT GU11 ....2 ...
Sidlaws Rd FARN GU14 ....28 ...
Silver Birch Cl FLEETS GU52 ....40 ...
Silverdale FLEETS GU52 ....40 ...
Silver Dr FRIM GU16 ....30 ...
Silverglades YTLY GU46 ....18 ...
Silver Hi SHST GU47 ....12 ...
Silver Park Cl FLEETS GU52 ....40 ...
Silverwood Dr CBLY GU15 ....15 ...
Silvester Wy FLEETS GU52 ....40 ...
Sine Cl FARN GU14 ....28 ...

rst Rd CBLY GU15...21 F2
Rd CHOB/PIR GU24...32 D2
l ALDT GU11...39 E5
d CBLY GU15...13 C5
y's Gn BFOR GU20...9 H4
glers' Wy FARN GU10...56 A5
ynch FNM GU9...5 J3
wood Rd FARN GU14...28 C2
drop Wy CHOB/PIR GU24...25 C4
s Paddock BFOR GU20...9 F1
s Ride BFOR GU20...9 H2
cron Rd FARN GU14...38 A1
rset Rd FARN GU14...28 B4
rville Crs YTLY GU46...11 E5
Av FNM GU9...48 B4
nge Cl SHST GU47...12 B5
t Dr LTWR GU18...15 H4
ampton Cl BLKW GU17...12 A5
ampton St FARN GU14...28 C4
Atlantic Dr ALDT GU11...3 G1
Av FNM GU9...48 B4
Beta Rd FARN GU14...38 A1
by Dr FLEETN GU51...35 H3
scote Dr CBLY GU15...22 C1
r CHOB/PIR GU24...32 C3
ern Rd CBLY GU15...13 C5
ern Wy FARN GU14...37 F1
Farm La BAGS GU19...16 H1
Gv FLEETS GU51...27 E5
lands Cl SHST GU47...50 C1
lands Rd ASHV GU12...50 C1
La ASHV GU12...50 D1
Meadow CWTH RG45...7 F5
mead Rd ALDT GU11...2 E6
ASHV GU12...44 B3
OB/PIR GU24...25 G5
CWTH RG45...7 C5
e Side RFNM GU10...50 B5
t FARN GU14...39 E5
eign Dr CBLY GU15...14 D4
owhawk Cl RFNM GU10...44 B2
eil Rd WOKN/KNAP GU21...33 H1
er Cl FLEETS GU52...30 A3
GU16...34 C4
pinney CBLY GU15...34 C4
EETN GU51...
La RFNM GU10...37 G4
La RFNM GU10...50 B5
 d Cl ALDT GU11...29 F1
gcross Av BLKW GU17...20 B3
gfield CWTH RG45...7 E2
gfield La FLEETN GU51...35 E3
gfield Rd ASHV GU12...44 C2
LY GU15...22 C1
g Gdns CBLY GU15...22 C1
glakes Est ASHV GU12 *...44 A4
g La FNM GU9...47 J3
g La West FNM GU9...47 G4
g Woods FLEETS GU52...35 F5
La West...12 A2
e Dr LTWR GU18...16 A4
e Wy FLEETN GU51...36 B5
Ct ALDT GU11...2 C4
pur WOKN/KNAP GU21...25 H5
rel Cl SHST GU47...11 H5
rel La FARN GU14...29 E4
res Drev CWTH RG45...6 B3
s cft BAGS GU19...15 F3
e Vw YTLY GU46...10 D4
College Rd CBLY GU15...13 F5
rd Lake CHOB/PIR GU24...25 G5
rd La FARN GU14...29 E5
ford Av FRIM GU16...22 B5
ope Rd CBLY GU15...22 D2
ey Dr FARN GU14 *...37 E1
ey Hl CHOB/PIR GU24...32 C4
on Dr FLEETS GU51...35 E4
s ASHV GU12...44 B5
Post Rd CBLY GU15...14 A3
an Ap ASHV GU12...39 C5
KW GU17...20 C2
NM GU10...5 H4
n Rd East ASHV GU12...3 G5
n Vw ASHV GU12...39 G5
s Rd ALDT GU11...43 F5
Forth Copse SHST GU47...12 C1
endale Rd FNM GU9...48 B4
ns Hl YTLY GU46...19 E1
ards Ri RFNM GU10...56 B1
e Down FRIM GU16...31 F1
ell Cl YTLY GU46...11 E5
g Cl ASHV GU12...44 B2
M GU16...24 A2
g Wy FARN GU14...37 F5
bridge Dr ALDT GU11...2 D4
abridge Wy YTLY GU46...18 D2
ton Av FLEETS GU52...35 F2
ton Pk FLEETN GU51...35 F2
wood Ri CBLY GU15...22 B4
wood Wy FNM GU9...48 C5
Hills FNM GU9...5 J1
gate Cl CBLY GU15...15 E5
hill Rd LTWR GU18...16 A2
house Ri FRIM GU16...31 F1
eleigh Ct FRIM GU16...30 A3
st ASHV GU12...3 K6

Stoney Cl YTLY GU46...18 D2
Stoneyfields FNM GU9...54 C4
Stookes Wy YTLY GU46...18 B2
Stourhead Cl FARN GU14...29 H5
Stovold's Wy ALDT GU11...2 A6
Stratford Rd ASHV GU12...39 F4
Stratton Wk FARN GU14...29 E2
Strawberry Cl CHOB/PIR GU24...32 D5
Strawberry Ct FRIM GU16...31 F1
Strawberry Flds
  CHOB/PIR GU24...25 G2
Strawberry Ri CHOB/PIR GU24...25 G2
Stream Farm Cl RFNM GU10...61 F1
Streamside FLEETN GU51...35 G4
Stream Valley Rd FARN GU10...61 E2
Streets Heath CHOB/PIR GU24...17 H4
The Street FARN GU14...40 A2
  RFNM GU10...50 B5
  RFNM GU10...60 A2
  RFNM GU10...62 A5
  RFNM GU10...63 G4
Stuart Cl FARN GU14...29 E3
Stubbs Folly SHST GU47...12 B4
Stubbs Moor Rd FARN GU14...28 D4
Sturdee Cl FRIM GU16...22 A5
Sturt Rd FNM GU9...4 H5
  FRIM GU16...30 B4
Suffield La RGUW GU3...57 H5
Suffolk Cl BAGS GU19...15 G1
Suffolk Ct FRIM GU16...31 F1
Sullivan Cl FARN GU14...29 H4
Sullivan Rd ALDT GU11...3 H6
Summerfield La RFNM GU10...62 C1
Summer Gdns FARN GU14...23 E1
Summit Av FARN GU14...37 E1
Sumner Rd FNM GU9...5 H1
Sundew Cl LTWR GU18...16 D5
Sunninghill Rd FARN GU9...9 E1
Sunnybank Ms ASHV GU12 *...44 D4
Sunnybank Rd FARN GU14...28 B5
Sunnydell La FNM GU9...60 C2
Sunny Hill Rd ALDT GU11...42 B5
Sunnyside FLEETN GU51...35 E2
  WOKN/KNAP GU21 *...33 H1
Sunnyview Cl ASHV GU12...3 H4
Sun Ray Est SHST GU47...11 F3
Surbiton Cl FRIM GU16...30 A5
Surrey Av CBLY GU15...21 E2
Surridge Ct BAGS GU19...15 G1
Sussex Gdns FLEETN GU51...26 D5
Sutton Rd CBLY GU15...14 C2
Swaledale Gdns FLEETN GU51...35 H1
Swale Rd FARN GU14...28 B5
Swallow Cl YTLY GU46...10 B5
Swan La SHST GU47...11 H5
Swan Wy FLEETN GU51...34 D5
Sweetbriar CWTH RG45 *...6 C1
Swift La BAGS GU19...15 H1
Swift Rd FNM GU9...47 H5
Swift's Cl RFNM GU10...55 F4
Swingate Rd FNM GU9...54 A5
Swiss Cl RFNM GU10...60 B4
Switchback La RFNM GU10...60 C5
Swordfish Wy FARN GU14...37 G5
Swordsman's Rd FRIM GU16...23 F5
Sycamore Cl FARN GU14...29 H5
  SHST GU47...11 H4
Sycamore Crs FLEETN GU51...40 A1
Sycamore Dr ASHV GU12...39 F5
  FRIM GU16...22 A4
  RFNM GU10...60 C2
Sycamore Rd FARN GU14...38 D2
The Sycamores BLKW GU17...19 H1
  FARN GU14...29 H5
Sydney Cl CWTH RG45...7 E1
Sydney Loader Pl BLKW GU17...11 G5
Sydney Smith Av FARN GU14...38 B3
Sylvan Rdg SHST GU47...11 G2
Sylvan Wy FLEETS GU52...40 B2
Sylvia Ct CHOB/PIR GU24...25 G2
Syon Pl FARN GU14...29 H5

Thompsons Cl CHOB/PIR GU24...32 D5
Thorburn Cha SHST GU47...12 C5
Thornbury Cl CWTH RG45...6 D3
Thorn Cl RFNM GU10...60 B4
Thorndown La BFOR GU20...9 H5
Thorne Cl CWTH RG45...6 C1
Thornhill Rd ALDT GU11...43 H3
Thorn Rd RFNM GU10...60 B4
Thornyhurst Rd FRIM GU16...30 C5
Thorold Rd FNM GU9...5 G2
Three Castles Pth HTWY RG27...10 A4
Three Stiles Rd FNM GU9...4 B2
Threshers Cnr FLEETN GU51...27 E5
Throgmorton Rd YTLY GU46...18 A1
Thundery Hl RFNM GU10...56 B1
Thurbans Rd FNM GU9...60 C1
Thyme Ct FARN GU14...28 A4
Tichborne Cl BLKW GU17...20 B1
Tichborne Pl ASHV GU12...3 J7
Tichbourne Cl FRIM GU16...22 A5
Tile Barn Cl FARN GU14...29 E3
Tilford Rd FNM GU9...5 J5
Timber Bank FRIM GU16...30 C4
Timber Cl FNM GU9 *...4 E5
Timberley Pl CWTH RG45...6 A4
Tindal Ct FARN GU14...10 D5
Tintagel Dr FRIM GU16...22 B5
Tisbury Ct FLEETN GU51...35 E1
Toad La BLKW GU17...20 C2
Toipuddle Wy YTLY GU46...19 H1
Tomlins Av FRIM GU16...22 B4
Tomlinscote Wy FRIM GU16...22 C4
Tongham Mdw RFNM GU10...50 A3
Tongham Rd ASHV GU12...3 J7
The Topiary FARN GU14...57 G1
Topiady Pl FNM GU9...4 B4
Top Terrace Rd FARN GU14...38 A4
Tor Rd FNM GU9...4 B4
Totford La FNM GU9...57 G2
Totland Ct FARN GU14...29 E3
Tottenham Wk SHST GU47...12 C5
Tournai Cl ALDT GU11...39 E5
Tower Hl FARN GU14...38 A1
Towers Dr CWTH RG45...6 D4
Townside Pl CBLY GU15...13 H5
Trafalgar Ct FARN GU14...38 B3
Trafalgar Wy CBLY GU15...20 D2
Trafford Rd FRIM GU16...29 H1
Transport Rd FARN GU14...38 B3
Travis La SHST GU47...12 B4
Trebor Av FNM GU9...5 H5
Tredenham Ct FARN GU14...38 C4
Treeside Dr FNM GU9...48 C5
Tree Tops Av CBLY GU15...14 C3
Tremayne Wk CBLY GU15...23 E2
Trent Cl FARN GU14...28 C3
Trenton Cl FRIM GU16...22 C4
Tresham Crs YTLY GU46...10 A5
Trimmers Cl FNM GU9...47 H5
Trimmers Fld FNM GU9...54 C4
Trimmers Rd FNM GU9...47 H5
Trinity SHST GU47...12 A3
Trinity Flds SHST GU47...47 G4
Trinity Hl FNM GU9...47 G4
Trinity St WOKN/KNAP GU21...25 H5
Trotsford Meadow
  BLKW GU17...20 A2
Trotwood Cl SHST GU47...12 C1
Trunk Rd FARN GU14...28 A5
Tudor Dr YTLY GU46...18 D2
Tudor Wy FLEETS GU52...40 C3
Tunnel Rd FARN GU14...37 G5
Tunworth Ct FLEETN GU51...34 D5
Turf Hill Rd CBLY GU15...14 B5
Turgis Rd FLEETN GU51...26 A5
Turner Pl SHST GU47...12 B5
Turners Av FLEETN GU51...26 A5
Turners Wy FLEETN GU51...26 A5
Turnstone End YTLY GU46...10 B5
Turnville Cl LTWR GU18...16 A2
Turpins Rd BFOR GU20...9 F2
Tuscany Wy YTLY GU46...18 C2
Tweed Cl FARN GU14...28 C3
Tweedsmuir Cl FARN GU14...37 F1
Twelve Acre Crs FARN GU14...28 B4
Tweseldown Rd FLEETS GU52...40 D3
Twisell Thorne FLEETS GU52...40 A3
Twyford La RFNM GU10...60 D2
Tyne Cl FARN GU14...28 C3

Ullswater Av FARN GU14...37 F1
Ullswater Cl FNM GU9...47 G4
  LTWR GU18...16 B2
Ullswater Ct ASHV GU12 *...44 B2
Ullswater Rd LTWR GU18...16 B2
Underhill La FNM GU9...60 D1
Underwood Av ASHV GU12...50 A1
Union Cl SHST GU47...12 C1
Union Rd FNM GU9...5 G4
  FRIM GU16...31 F1
Union St ALDT GU11...3 F1
  CHOB/PIR GU24...32 A3
  FARN GU14...29 E5
Updown Hl BFOR GU20...9 H4
Upland Rd CBLY GU15...14 B3
Uplands Cl SHST GU47...11 H5
Uplands Rd FARN GU14...54 C4
Upper Bourne La RFNM GU10...60 C2
Upper Bourne V RFNM GU10...60 C3
Upper Broadmoor Rd
  CWTH RG45...7 F3
Upper Charles St CBLY GU15...13 G5
Upper Chobham Rd
  CBLY GU15...22 D2
Upper Church La FNM GU9...5 F4
Upper College Ride
  CBLY GU15...14 A3
Upper Elms Rd ALDT GU11...2 C4
Upper Froyle Dr FLEETN GU51...34 D1

Upper Gordon Rd CBLY GU15...21 H1
Upper Hale Rd FNM GU9...47 H3
Upper Old Park La FNM GU9...47 F5
Upper Park Rd CBLY GU15...21 H1
Upper Pinewood Rd
  ASHV GU12...45 E4
Upper St Michael's Rd
  ALDT GU11...2 E6
Upper South Vw FNM GU9...5 G2
Upper St FLEETN GU51...35 F5
Upper Terrace Rd FARN GU14...38 A4
Upper Union St ALDT GU11...2 B3
Upper Union Ter ALDT GU11...2 C3
Upper Verran Rd CBLY GU15...21 H3
Upper Wy FNM GU9...53 H5
Upper Weybourne La
  FNM GU9...48 B2
Upper Wield Dr FLEETN GU51...26 A5
Upton Cl FARN GU14...38 D1

Vale Cl RFNM GU10...61 E4
Vale Rd ASHV GU12...39 G5
  CBLY GU15...21 E2
Vale Wood Dr RFNM GU10...61 E4
Valiant Wy FARN GU14...37 H4
Valley La FNM GU9...60 D1
Valley Rd FRIM GU16...30 D1
Valley Vw SHST GU47...11 G4
Valroy Cl FARN GU14...13 H5
Vampire Wy FARN GU14...37 G4
Vapery La CHOB/PIR GU24...24 B4
Varney Cl FARN GU14...28 C4
Velmead Cl FLEETS GU52...35 H5
Velmead Rd FLEETS GU52...35 G5
Ventnor Ter ASHV GU12...3 G5
Verge Wk ALDT GU11...42 B5
The Verne FLEETS GU52...40 C2
Verran Rd CBLY GU15...21 H4
Vesey Cl FARN GU14...29 E4
Viburnum Ct CHOB/PIR GU24...17 E5
Vicarage Ct FNM GU9...48 B4
Vicarage Gdns FLEETS GU52...40 B5
Vicarage Hi FNM GU9...61 D1
Vicarage La FNM GU9...5 F4
  FNM GU9...48 A3
  YTLY GU46...18 C3
Vicarage Rd BFOR GU20...8 A5
  BLKW GU17...20 C2
  YTLY GU46...10 C4
Vickers Rd ASHV GU12...44 B2
Victoria Av FARN GU14...37 F4
Victoria Ct BAGS GU19...15 G2
Victoria Dr BLKW GU17...20 A2
Victoria Gdns FLEETN GU51...35 H3
Victoria Hill Rd FLEETN GU51...35 E3
Victoria Ms FLEETN GU51 *...35 F3
Victoria Pde FLEETN GU51 *...35 F3
Victoria Rd ALDT GU11...2 D5
  FARN GU14...29 F5
  FLEETN GU51...35 E3
  FNM GU9...5 G4
Victoria Tr ALDT GU11...37 F5
Victor Wy FARN GU14...37 F4
Vigo La YTLY GU46...18 C1
Village Wy YTLY GU46...10 D4
Vine Cl ALDT GU11...43 E1
  RFNM GU10...60 C1
Vine House Cl FRIM GU16...39 D1
Vine St ALDT GU11...2 C4
Vine Wy FNM GU9...60 C5
Vintney St FLEETN GU51...34 D1
Virginia Gdns FARN GU14...38 B2
Viscount Ct ASHV GU12...44 B2
Vivian Cl FLEETS GU52...40 D1
Vulcan Wy FARN GU14...37 E4
  SHST GU47...11 G4

Wadham SHST GU47...12 D2
Waggoners Hollow BAGS GU19...15 G1
Wakefords Copse
  FLEETS GU52...40 D4
Wakefords Cnr FLEETS GU52 *...40 D3
Wakefords Pk FLEETS GU52...40 D4
Waldort Hts ALDT GU17...20 B2
Walker's Rdg CBLY GU15...22 A1
Wallace Wy ALDT GU11...2 A1
Wallington Ct CBLY GU15...14 C2
Waimer Cl CWTH RG45...7 E3
  FRIM GU16...30 B2
Walnut Cl ALDT GU11...2 D7
  YTLY GU46...18 D2
Walrus Rd FARN GU14...37 H4
Waltham Cl SHST GU47...12 B2
Walton Cl ASHV GU12...3 H5
Wandsdyke Cl FRIM GU16...30 B1
Wantage Rd SHST GU47...12 B3
Wapiti Wy FARN GU14...37 H4
Wardle Cl BAGS GU19...15 H1
Wargrove Dr SHST GU47...12 B5
Warren Cl FLEETS GU52...40 A3
  SHST GU47...11 G5
Warren Cnr RFNM GU10...46 C5
Warren Ri FRIM GU16...22 A3
The Warren ALDT GU11...2 B4
Warrington Ms ALDT GU11...48 C2
Warwick Cl ALDT GU11...3 G7
  CBLY GU15...22 D3
Warwick Rd ASHV GU12...39 F5
  FARN GU14...37 H4
Wasdale Cl SHST GU47...12 B4
Watchetts Dr CBLY GU15...21 G4
Watchetts Lake Cl CBLY GU15...21 H4
Watchetts Rd CBLY GU15...21 F3

Watchmoor Point
  CBLY GU15 *...21 F2
Watchmoor Rd CBLY GU15...21 E5
Waterhouse Md SHST GU47...12 B4
Water La CHOB/PIR GU24...33 E1
  FARN GU14...29 E2
  FNM GU9...54 D1
Waterloo Cl FARN GU14...14 D4
Waterloo Pl CWTH RG45 *...6 D4
Waterloo Rd ASHV GU12...3 G5
  CWTH RG45...6 C4
Water Rede FLEETS GU52...40 A4
Waterside Ct FLEETN GU51...35 H1
Waterside Ms FLEETN GU51...35 H1
Watery La FLEETS GU52...40 A4
Watts Common Rd ALDT GU17...37 G5
Watts Rd FARN GU14...28 D4
Waverley Av FLEETN GU51...35 F1
Waverley Cl CBLY GU15...22 B2
  FNM GU9...5 J4
Waverley Dr ASHV GU12...44 C1
  CBLY GU15...22 A1
Waverley Gdns FARN GU14...44 C1
Waverley La FNM GU9...5 K4
Waverley Rd BAGS GU19...8 B5
  FNM GU9...5 J5
Wayman Rd FARN GU14...28 C1
Waynflete La FNM GU9...54 B4
Ways End CBLY GU15...22 A2
Weaver Moss SHST GU47...11 H4
Weavers Gdns RFNM GU10...60 B3
Webb Cl BAGS GU19...15 G2
Weir Av FARN GU14...38 A1
Weir Cl FARN GU14...38 A1
Weir Rd FARN GU14...36 C2
Welbeck Cl FARN GU14...38 D3
Weldon Cl FLEETS GU52...40 D2
Wellburn Cl SHST GU47...11 H4
Well Cl CBLY GU15...21 F2
Weller Dr CBLY GU15...21 G5
Wellesley Cl ASHV GU12...45 E4
  BAGS GU19...8 A5
Wellesley Dr CWTH RG45...6 A5
Wellesley Gdn FARN GU14...48 A3
Wellesley Ga ASHV GU12 *...2 E4
Wellesley Rd ALDT GU11...2 B4
  FARN GU14...37 F4
Wellington Av ALDT GU11...3 H2
  FLEETN GU51...35 H2
Wellington Cl SHST GU47...12 A3
Wellington Gdns ALDT GU11 *...2 A4
Wellington La FNM GU9...48 B5
Wellington Pl ASHV GU12...44 B3
Wellington Rd CWTH RG45...7 E4
  SHST GU47...11 H5
Wellington St ALDT GU11...2 D2
Wellington Ter SHST GU47...12 A3
Wellington Wy FARN GU14...37 F5
Wells Cottages FNM GU9...60 C1
Wendover Dr FRIM GU16...23 E3
Wensleydale Dr CBLY GU15...23 H5
Wentworth Cl ASHV GU12...3 H5
  CWTH RG45...6 B2
  FNM GU9...48 D4
  YTLY GU46...18 D1
Wentworth Crs ASHV GU12...44 C1
Wessex Pl FNM GU9...5 H5
West Av FNM GU9...48 B4
Westbourne Rd SHST GU47...12 C4
Westbury Av FLEETS GU52...36 B4
Westbury Ct CWTH RG45...6 D2
  FLEETN GU51...36 A4
Westbury Gdns FLEETS GU52...36 B4
  FNM GU9...54 C1
Westbury Wy ASHV GU12...3 J2
West Cl FNM GU9...48 B3
West End Gv FNM GU9...4 A3
West End La RFNM GU10...62 A2
Westerdale Dr FRIM GU16...22 D3
Western Av CHOB/PIR GU24...33 C5
Western Rd ALDT GU11...48 C1
Westfield La RFNM GU10...60 A2
Westfield Rd CBLY GU15...21 F1
West Fryerne YTLY GU46...10 D4
Westglade FARN GU14...28 B5
West Gn YTLY GU46...10 B4
West Heath CHOB/PIR GU24...32 D5
West Heath Rd FARN GU14...28 D5
Westhill Cl CBLY GU15 *...24 D3
West Hill Gdns FLEETN GU51...34 D2
The West Hundreds
  FLEETN GU51...35 H1
Westmead FARN GU14...38 B1
West Md FNM GU9...4 E5
Westminster Cl FLEETN GU51...35 G2
Westmorland Dr CBLY GU15...22 D3
Weston Gv BAGS GU19...15 H1
Westover Rd FLEETS GU52...35 H5
West Rdg RFNM GU10...50 B5
West Ring RFNM GU10...50 B5
Westside Ct CHOB/PIR GU24 *...17 E5
West St FNM GU9...4 E4
Westwood Rd BFOR GU20...9 H4
Wetherby Gdns FARN GU14...38 C4
Wey Bank ALDT GU54...58 C5
Weybank Cl FNM GU9...5 H2
Weybourne Rd FNM GU9...48 C5
Weybridge Md YTLY GU46...11 E5
Weydon Farm La FNM GU9...5 F7
Weydon Hill Cl FNM GU9...5 F7
Weydon Hill Rd FNM GU9...5 F7
Weydon Mill La FNM GU9...4 E6
Weywood Cl FNM GU9...48 D5
Weywood La FNM GU9...48 C5
Wharfenden Wy FRIM GU16...30 B3
Wharf Rd FRIM GU16...30 B3
  FNM GU9...5 G4
Wharf Wy FRIM GU16...30 B3
Wheatley Rd ALDT GU11...2 B2
Whetstone Rd FARN GU14...28 B4
Whin Holt FLEETS GU52...40 C1

Index - featured places

op Kiln
M GU9 ....**5** F6
s Place Industrial Estate
Y GU15 ....**21** F3
ds Business Centre
F GU9 ....**54** D1
per's Lodge
ETN GU51 ....**27** G5
M GU16 ....**22** A3
gsaw School
M GU16 ....**39** E1
ll Court Business Park
Y GU15 ....**20** D2
ngs Centre
ST GU11 ....**2** D2
grove Industrial Estate
N GU14 ....**38** A1
International College
Y GU15 ....**21** G4
mead Shopping Centre
N GU14 ....**38** B1
ons Industrial Estate
.....................................**44** A5
ill Lower School
KN/KNAP GU21 ....**25** H5
Hill School
DB/PIR GU24 ....**33** E4
de Business Park
ST GU47 ....**11** G4
de Country Club
M GU16 ....**30** C3
de International Hotel
M GU16 ....**30** C3
de Primary School
M GU16 ....**22** B5
ater Country Park
VR GU18 ....**15** H2
ater Village School
VR GU18 ....**16** A2
rd Business Park
M GU16 ....**39** F1
Lamb Yard
pping Centre
M GU9 ....**4** E2
he Infant School
N GU14 ....**14** C2
urst School
Y GU15 ....**21** F1
Way Industrial Estate
M GU16 ....**11** C5
square Shopping Centre
Y GU15 ....**13** G5
Farm Business Centre
JM GU10 ....**50** B5
Park Industrial Estate
IV GU12 ....**3** G4
Primary School
N GU14 ....**28** D3
rough County
ant School *ALDT* GU11 ......**38** D3
eadows (Superstores)
T GU47 ....**20** C1

Middle Hill Health Clinic
ALDT GU11 ....**2** D1
Military Cemetery
CHOB/PIR GU24 ....**33** F3
More House School
RFNM GU10 ....**63** E1
Mytchett Primary School
M GU16 ....**30** B5
Newlands CP School
YTLY GU46 ....**18** C1
Newport Junior School
ASHV GU12 ....**3** J5
New Scotland Hill
Primary School
SHST GU47 ....**11** G1
North Farnborough County
Infant School *FARN* GU14 ......**29** H4
North Hants Golf Club
FLEETN GU51 ....**26** C5
Northtown Trading Estate
ASHV GU12 ....**50** A1
Oak Farm Community School
FARN GU14 ....**29** E3
Oaklands County J & I School
CWTH RG45 ....**6** C2
Oak Park Golf Club
RFNM GU10 ....**46** A4
Our Ladys Preparatory School
CWTH RG45 ....**6** C3
Owlsmoor Primary School
SHST GU47 ....**12** C2
Park Crematorium
ASHV GU12 ....**49** H4
Park Farm Industrial Estate
FRIM GU16 ....**21** G5
Park Primary School
FRIM GU16 ....**49** G3
Pennyhill Park Hotel
CBLY GU15 ....**14** D1
Pierreponte School
RFNM GU10 ....**63** G2
The Pilgrims Way
Primary School *FNM* GU9 ......**4** E7
Pine Ridge Golf Club
FRIM GU16 ....**23** F4
Pine Ridge Infant &
Nursery School *CBLY* GU15 ....**14** C2
Pinewood Infant School
FARN GU14 ....**28** B2
Pirbright Camp
CHOB/PIR GU24 ....**32** B2
Pirbright Primary School
CHOB/PIR GU24 ....**33** E4
Portesbery School
CBLY GU15 ....**13** H5
Potley Hill County
Primary School *BLKW* GU17 ....**19** G1
Potters Gate CE
Primary School
FNM GU9 ....**4** D3
Potters Industrial Park
FLEETS GU52 ....**41** E2

Potters International Hotel
ALDT GU11 ....**42** D3
Preymead Industrial Estate
FNM GU9 ....**49** F3
Prince Consort's Library
ALDT GU11 ....**42** D4
Princes Hall
ALDT GU11 ....**2** C2
Princes Mead Shopping Centre
FARN GU14 ....**38** B1
The Princess Royal Barracks
FRIM GU16 ....**31** F2
Prior Heath Infant School
CBLY GU15 ....**22** C1
Redfields Business Park
FLEETS GU52 ....**40** A5
The Ridgeway Community
School *FNM* GU9 ....**61** E1
Riverside Park Industrial Estate
FNM GU9 ....**5** J2
Romans Business Park
FNM GU9 ....**5** J1
Rowledge CE (Controlled)
Primary School
RFNM GU10 ....**59** H5
Royal Army Medical Corps
ALDT GU11 ....**43** H3
Royal Logistic Corps Museum
FRIM GU16 ....**31** F1
Royal Military Academy
CBLY GU15 ....**12** D5
Rural Life Centre
RFNM GU10 ....**61** H5
St Andrews CE Infant School
FNM GU9 ....**5** F4
St Bernadettes County Primary
School *FARN* GU14 ....**29** E4
St Georges Industrial Estate
CBLY GU15 ....**21** F3
St Josephs Catholic Primary
School *ALDT* GU11 ....**2** D7
St Marks CE Primary
School
FARN GU14 ....**38** D4
St Marys CE Aided
Infant School
RFNM GU10 ....**63** F4
St Michaels Abbey
FARN GU14 ....**29** G4
St Michaels CE Infant School
ALDT GU11 ....**3** F7
St Michaels CE Junior School
ALDT GU11 ....**3** G7
St Michaels CE Primary School
SHST GU47 ....**11** E3
St Nicholas School
FLEETS GU52 ....**40** A5
St Omer Barracks
ALDT GU11 ....**43** H3
St Patricks Catholic
Primary School
FARN GU14 ....**29** H5

St Pauls CE Infant School
RFNM GU10 ....**50** C3
St Peters CE (Aided)
Primary School *FNM* GU9 ......**60** B1
St Peters CE Junior School
FARN GU14 ....**29** C5
YTLY GU46 ....**10** D5
St Polycarps Catholic
Primary School *FNM* GU9 ......**5** J5
Salesian College
FARN GU14 ....**38** D3
Sampson Business Park
FARN GU14 ....**21** F3
The Samuel Cody School
ALDT GU11 ....**38** B5
Sandhurst School
SHST GU47 ....**12** B2
Sandhurst Sports Club
SHST GU47 ....**12** A4
Shawfield Primary School
ASHV GU12 ....**44** C4
The Sixth Form College
FARN GU14 ....**29** F2
South Farnborough
County Junior School
FARN GU14 ....**38** D2
South Farnborough
Infant School *FARN* GU14 ......**38** D4
South Farnham Middle School
FNM GU9 ....**54** C4
Southwood Golf Club
FARN GU14 ....**37** G2
Springlake Country Club
ASHV GU12 ....**44** A3
Station Industrial Estate
FLEETN GU51 ....**35** H1
Stubbs Industrial Estate
ALDT GU11 ....**44** A2
Surrey Heath Museum
CBLY GU15 ....**13** H5
Surrey Institute of Art & Design
FNM GU9 ....**4** E3
Talavera Primary School
ALDT GU11 ....**2** D1
Tavistock Infant School
FLEETN GU51 ....**34** D4
Tennis Club
FLEETS GU52 ....**40** B4
Thomson House
FARN GU14 ....**29** C4
Tomlinscote School
FRIM GU16 ....**22** B4
Tower Hill Primary School
FARN GU14 ....**37** H1
Travel Inn
BAGS GU19 ....**8** C3
FARN GU14 ....**37** G1
FARN GU14 ....**12** B4
Trilakes Country Park
SHST GU47 ....**11** F4
Tweseldown Infant School
FLEETS GU52 ....**40** D3

Uplands CP School
SHST GU47 ....**11** H3
Walsh CE First & Middle School
ASHV GU12 ....**50** B1
The Watchetts Junior School
CBLY GU15 ....**21** G4
Waterfront Business Park
FLEETN GU51 ....**35** H2
The Wavell Technology College
ALDT GU11 ....**38** B5
Waverley Abbey House
FNM GU9 ....**55** F5
Wellington Business Park
CWTH RG45 ....**6** A4
Wellington College
CWTH RG45 ....**6** C4
Wellington Shopping Centre
ALDT GU11 ....**2** D3
Wellington Sports Centre
CWTH RG45 ....**6** B4
West End Infant School
ALDT GU11 ....**2** B4
Westfields Primary School
YTLY GU46 ....**18** B1
West Hill Golf Club
CHOB/PIR GU24 ....**33** H3
Weybourne County
Infant School
FNM GU9 ....**48** C4
Weydon County Secondary
School *FNM* GU9 ....**60** B1
William Cobbett Junior School
FNM GU9 ....**48** C4
Windlemere Golf Club
CHOB/PIR GU24 ....**17** E3
Windlesham Golf Club
BAGS GU19 ....**8** D4
Windlesham Village
Infant School *BFOR* GU20 ......**9** E2
Woodcote House School
BFOR GU20 ....**9** F3
Wyke CP School
RGUW GU3 ....**45** H3
Yateley Common
Country Park *BLKW* GU17 ......**19** F3
Yateley Health Centre
YTLY GU46 ....**10** D5
Yateley Infant School
YTLY GU46 ....**10** D5
Yateley Manor Preparatory
School *YTLY* GU46 ....**10** D5
Yateley School & Sixth
Form Centre *YTLY* GU46 ......**18** C1
York Town Industrial Estate
CBLY GU15 ....**21** E1

Acknowledgements

ost Office is a registered trademark of Post Office Ltd. in the UK and other countries.

ols address data provided by Education Direct.

station information supplied by Johnsons

way street data provided by © Tele Atlas N.V. Tele Atlas

en centre information provided by

en Centre Association   Britains best garden centres

ale Garden Centres

tatement on the front cover of this atlas is sourced, selected and quoted
a reader comment and feedback form received in 2004.

Notes

Notes

Notes

 **Street by Street** QUESTIONNAIRE

Dear Atlas User
Your comments, opinions and recommendations are very important to us.
So please help us to improve our street atlases by taking a few minutes
to complete this simple questionnaire.

You do not need a stamp (unless posted outside the UK). If you do not want to remove
this page from your street atlas, then photocopy it or write your answers on a plain sheet
of paper.

Send to: The Editor, AA Street by Street, FREEPOST SCE 4598,
Basingstoke RG21 4GY

ABOUT THE ATLAS...

Which city/town/county did you buy?

Are there any features of the atlas or mapping that you find particularly useful?

Is there anything we could have done better?

Why did you choose an AA Street by Street atlas?

Did it meet your expectations?

Exceeded ☐   **Met all** ☐   **Met most** ☐   **Fell below** ☐

Please give your reasons

Where did you buy it?

For what purpose? (please tick all applicable)

To use in your own local area ☐　To use on business or at work ☐

Visiting a strange place ☐　In the car ☐　On foot ☐

Other (please state)

LOCAL KNOWLEDGE...

Local knowledge is invaluable. Whilst every attempt has been made to make the information contained in this atlas as accurate as possible, should you notice any inaccuracies, please detail them below (if necessary, use a blank piece of paper) or e-mail us at *streetbystreet@theAA.com*

ABOUT YOU...

Name (Mr/Mrs/Ms)
Address
　　　　　　　　　　　　　　　　　　　　　　　Postcode
Daytime tel no
E-mail address

Which age group are you in?

Under 25 ☐　**25-34** ☐　**35-44** ☐　**45-54** ☐　**55-64** ☐　**65+** ☐

Are you an AA member?　YES ☐　NO ☐

Do you have Internet access?　YES ☐　NO ☐

Thank you for taking the time to complete this questionnaire. Please send it to us as soon as possible, and remember, you do not need a stamp (unless posted outside the UK).

We may want to contact you about other products and services provided by us, or our partners (by mail, telephone) but please tick the box if you DO NOT wish to hear about such products and services from us by mail or telephone. ☐

ML164z